Hannah Arendt: A Very Short Introduction

VERY SHORT INTRODUCTIONS are for anyone wanting a stimulating and accessible way into a new subject. They are written by experts, and have been translated into more than 45 different languages.

The series began in 1995, and now covers a wide variety of topics in every discipline. The VSI library currently contains over 700 volumes—a Very Short Introduction to everything from Psychology and Philosophy of Science to American History and Relativity—and continues to grow in every subject area.

Very Short Introductions available now:

ABOLITIONISM Richard S. Newman
THE ABRAHAMIC RELIGIONS Charles L. Cohen
ACCOUNTING Christopher Nobes
ADOLESCENCE Peter K. Smith
THEODOR W. ADORNO Andrew Bowie
ADVERTISING Winston Fletcher
AERIAL WARFARE Frank Ledwidge
AESTHETICS Bence Nanay
AFRICAN AMERICAN RELIGION Eddie S. Glaude Jr
AFRICAN HISTORY John Parker and Richard Rathbone
AFRICAN POLITICS Ian Taylor
AFRICAN RELIGIONS Jacob K. Olupona
AGEING Nancy A. Pachana
AGNOSTICISM Robin Le Poidevin
AGRICULTURE Paul Brassley and Richard Soffe
ALEXANDER THE GREAT Hugh Bowden
ALGEBRA Peter M. Higgins
AMERICAN BUSINESS HISTORY Walter A. Friedman
AMERICAN CULTURAL HISTORY Eric Avila
AMERICAN FOREIGN RELATIONS Andrew Preston
AMERICAN HISTORY Paul S. Boyer
AMERICAN IMMIGRATION David A. Gerber
AMERICAN INTELLECTUAL HISTORY Jennifer Ratner-Rosenhagen
THE AMERICAN JUDICIAL SYSTEM Charles L. Zelden
AMERICAN LEGAL HISTORY G. Edward White
AMERICAN MILITARY HISTORY Joseph T. Glatthaar
AMERICAN NAVAL HISTORY Craig L. Symonds
AMERICAN POETRY David Caplan
AMERICAN POLITICAL HISTORY Donald Critchlow
AMERICAN POLITICAL PARTIES AND ELECTIONS L. Sandy Maisel
AMERICAN POLITICS Richard M. Valelly
THE AMERICAN PRESIDENCY Charles O. Jones
THE AMERICAN REVOLUTION Robert J. Allison
AMERICAN SLAVERY Heather Andrea Williams
THE AMERICAN SOUTH Charles Reagan Wilson
THE AMERICAN WEST Stephen Aron
AMERICAN WOMEN'S HISTORY Susan Ware
AMPHIBIANS T. S. Kemp
ANAESTHESIA Aidan O'Donnell
ANALYTIC PHILOSOPHY Michael Beaney
ANARCHISM Alex Prichard

ANCIENT ASSYRIA Karen Radner
ANCIENT EGYPT Ian Shaw
ANCIENT EGYPTIAN ART AND ARCHITECTURE Christina Riggs
ANCIENT GREECE Paul Cartledge
THE ANCIENT NEAR EAST Amanda H. Podany
ANCIENT PHILOSOPHY Julia Annas
ANCIENT WARFARE Harry Sidebottom
ANGELS David Albert Jones
ANGLICANISM Mark Chapman
THE ANGLO-SAXON AGE John Blair
ANIMAL BEHAVIOUR Tristram D. Wyatt
THE ANIMAL KINGDOM Peter Holland
ANIMAL RIGHTS David DeGrazia
THE ANTARCTIC Klaus Dodds
ANTHROPOCENE Erle C. Ellis
ANTISEMITISM Steven Beller
ANXIETY Daniel Freeman and Jason Freeman
THE APOCRYPHAL GOSPELS Paul Foster
APPLIED MATHEMATICS Alain Goriely
THOMAS AQUINAS Fergus Kerr
ARBITRATION Thomas Schultz and Thomas Grant
ARCHAEOLOGY Paul Bahn
ARCHITECTURE Andrew Ballantyne
THE ARCTIC Klaus Dodds and Jamie Woodward
HANNAH ARENDT Dana Villa
ARISTOCRACY William Doyle
ARISTOTLE Jonathan Barnes
ART HISTORY Dana Arnold
ART THEORY Cynthia Freeland
ARTIFICIAL INTELLIGENCE Margaret A. Boden
ASIAN AMERICAN HISTORY Madeline Y. Hsu
ASTROBIOLOGY David C. Catling
ASTROPHYSICS James Binney
ATHEISM Julian Baggini
THE ATMOSPHERE Paul I. Palmer
AUGUSTINE Henry Chadwick
JANE AUSTEN Tom Keymer
AUSTRALIA Kenneth Morgan
AUTISM Uta Frith
AUTOBIOGRAPHY Laura Marcus
THE AVANT GARDE David Cottington
THE AZTECS Davíd Carrasco
BABYLONIA Trevor Bryce
BACTERIA Sebastian G. B. Amyes
BANKING John Goddard and John O. S. Wilson
BARTHES Jonathan Culler
THE BEATS David Sterritt
BEAUTY Roger Scruton
LUDWIG VAN BEETHOVEN Mark Evan Bonds
BEHAVIOURAL ECONOMICS Michelle Baddeley
BESTSELLERS John Sutherland
THE BIBLE John Riches
BIBLICAL ARCHAEOLOGY Eric H. Cline
BIG DATA Dawn E. Holmes
BIOCHEMISTRY Mark Lorch
BIOGEOGRAPHY Mark V. Lomolino
BIOGRAPHY Hermione Lee
BIOMETRICS Michael Fairhurst
ELIZABETH BISHOP Jonathan F. S. Post
BLACK HOLES Katherine Blundell
BLASPHEMY Yvonne Sherwood
BLOOD Chris Cooper
THE BLUES Elijah Wald
THE BODY Chris Shilling
NIELS BOHR J. L. Heilbron
THE BOOK OF COMMON PRAYER Brian Cummings
THE BOOK OF MORMON Terryl Givens
BORDERS Alexander C. Diener and Joshua Hagen
THE BRAIN Michael O'Shea
BRANDING Robert Jones
THE BRICS Andrew F. Cooper
THE BRITISH CONSTITUTION Martin Loughlin
THE BRITISH EMPIRE Ashley Jackson
BRITISH POLITICS Tony Wright
BUDDHA Michael Carrithers
BUDDHISM Damien Keown
BUDDHIST ETHICS Damien Keown
BYZANTIUM Peter Sarris
CALVINISM Jon Balserak
ALBERT CAMUS Oliver Gloag

CANADA Donald Wright
CANCER Nicholas James
CAPITALISM James Fulcher
CATHOLICISM Gerald O'Collins
CAUSATION Stephen Mumford and Rani Lill Anjum
THE CELL Terence Allen and Graham Cowling
THE CELTS Barry Cunliffe
CHAOS Leonard Smith
GEOFFREY CHAUCER David Wallace
CHEMISTRY Peter Atkins
CHILD PSYCHOLOGY Usha Goswami
CHILDREN'S LITERATURE Kimberley Reynolds
CHINESE LITERATURE Sabina Knight
CHOICE THEORY Michael Allingham
CHRISTIAN ART Beth Williamson
CHRISTIAN ETHICS D. Stephen Long
CHRISTIANITY Linda Woodhead
CIRCADIAN RHYTHMS Russell Foster and Leon Kreitzman
CITIZENSHIP Richard Bellamy
CITY PLANNING Carl Abbott
CIVIL ENGINEERING David Muir Wood
CLASSICAL LITERATURE William Allan
CLASSICAL MYTHOLOGY Helen Morales
CLASSICS Mary Beard and John Henderson
CLAUSEWITZ Michael Howard
CLIMATE Mark Maslin
CLIMATE CHANGE Mark Maslin
CLINICAL PSYCHOLOGY Susan Llewelyn and Katie Aafjes-van Doorn
COGNITIVE BEHAVIOURAL THERAPY Freda McManus
COGNITIVE NEUROSCIENCE Richard Passingham
THE COLD WAR Robert J. McMahon
COLONIAL AMERICA Alan Taylor
COLONIAL LATIN AMERICAN LITERATURE Rolena Adorno
COMBINATORICS Robin Wilson
COMEDY Matthew Bevis
COMMUNISM Leslie Holmes
COMPARATIVE LITERATURE Ben Hutchinson
COMPETITION AND ANTITRUST LAW Ariel Ezrachi
COMPLEXITY John H. Holland
THE COMPUTER Darrel Ince
COMPUTER SCIENCE Subrata Dasgupta
CONCENTRATION CAMPS Dan Stone
CONFUCIANISM Daniel K. Gardner
THE CONQUISTADORS Matthew Restall and Felipe Fernández-Armesto
CONSCIENCE Paul Strohm
CONSCIOUSNESS Susan Blackmore
CONTEMPORARY ART Julian Stallabrass
CONTEMPORARY FICTION Robert Eaglestone
CONTINENTAL PHILOSOPHY Simon Critchley
COPERNICUS Owen Gingerich
CORAL REEFS Charles Sheppard
CORPORATE SOCIAL RESPONSIBILITY Jeremy Moon
CORRUPTION Leslie Holmes
COSMOLOGY Peter Coles
COUNTRY MUSIC Richard Carlin
CREATIVITY Vlad Glăveanu
CRIME FICTION Richard Bradford
CRIMINAL JUSTICE Julian V. Roberts
CRIMINOLOGY Tim Newburn
CRITICAL THEORY Stephen Eric Bronner
THE CRUSADES Christopher Tyerman
CRYPTOGRAPHY Fred Piper and Sean Murphy
CRYSTALLOGRAPHY A. M. Glazer
THE CULTURAL REVOLUTION Richard Curt Kraus
DADA AND SURREALISM David Hopkins
DANTE Peter Hainsworth and David Robey
DARWIN Jonathan Howard
THE DEAD SEA SCROLLS Timothy H. Lim
DECADENCE David Weir
DECOLONIZATION Dane Kennedy
DEMENTIA Kathleen Taylor
DEMOCRACY Bernard Crick

DEMOGRAPHY Sarah Harper
DEPRESSION Jan Scott and Mary Jane Tacchi
DERRIDA Simon Glendinning
DESCARTES Tom Sorell
DESERTS Nick Middleton
DESIGN John Heskett
DEVELOPMENT Ian Goldin
DEVELOPMENTAL BIOLOGY Lewis Wolpert
THE DEVIL Darren Oldridge
DIASPORA Kevin Kenny
CHARLES DICKENS Jenny Hartley
DICTIONARIES Lynda Mugglestone
DINOSAURS David Norman
DIPLOMATIC HISTORY Joseph M. Siracusa
DOCUMENTARY FILM Patricia Aufderheide
DREAMING J. Allan Hobson
DRUGS Les Iversen
DRUIDS Barry Cunliffe
DYNASTY Jeroen Duindam
DYSLEXIA Margaret J. Snowling
EARLY MUSIC Thomas Forrest Kelly
THE EARTH Martin Redfern
EARTH SYSTEM SCIENCE Tim Lenton
ECOLOGY Jaboury Ghazoul
ECONOMICS Partha Dasgupta
EDUCATION Gary Thomas
EGYPTIAN MYTH Geraldine Pinch
EIGHTEENTH-CENTURY BRITAIN Paul Langford
THE ELEMENTS Philip Ball
EMOTION Dylan Evans
EMPIRE Stephen Howe
EMPLOYMENT LAW David Cabrelli
ENERGY SYSTEMS Nick Jenkins
ENGELS Terrell Carver
ENGINEERING David Blockley
THE ENGLISH LANGUAGE Simon Horobin
ENGLISH LITERATURE Jonathan Bate
THE ENLIGHTENMENT John Robertson
ENTREPRENEURSHIP Paul Westhead and Mike Wright
ENVIRONMENTAL ECONOMICS Stephen Smith
ENVIRONMENTAL ETHICS Robin Attfield
ENVIRONMENTAL LAW Elizabeth Fisher
ENVIRONMENTAL POLITICS Andrew Dobson
ENZYMES Paul Engel
EPICUREANISM Catherine Wilson
EPIDEMIOLOGY Rodolfo Saracci
ETHICS Simon Blackburn
ETHNOMUSICOLOGY Timothy Rice
THE ETRUSCANS Christopher Smith
EUGENICS Philippa Levine
THE EUROPEAN UNION Simon Usherwood and John Pinder
EUROPEAN UNION LAW Anthony Arnull
EVANGELICALISM John Stackhouse
EVIL Luke Russell
EVOLUTION Brian and Deborah Charlesworth
EXISTENTIALISM Thomas Flynn
EXPLORATION Stewart A. Weaver
EXTINCTION Paul B. Wignall
THE EYE Michael Land
FAIRY TALE Marina Warner
FAMILY LAW Jonathan Herring
MICHAEL FARADAY Frank A. J. L. James
FASCISM Kevin Passmore
FASHION Rebecca Arnold
FEDERALISM Mark J. Rozell and Clyde Wilcox
FEMINISM Margaret Walters
FILM Michael Wood
FILM MUSIC Kathryn Kalinak
FILM NOIR James Naremore
FIRE Andrew C. Scott
THE FIRST WORLD WAR Michael Howard
FLUID MECHANICS Eric Lauga
FOLK MUSIC Mark Slobin
FOOD John Krebs
FORENSIC PSYCHOLOGY David Canter
FORENSIC SCIENCE Jim Fraser
FORESTS Jaboury Ghazoul
FOSSILS Keith Thomson
FOUCAULT Gary Gutting
THE FOUNDING FATHERS R. B. Bernstein

FRACTALS Kenneth Falconer
FREE SPEECH Nigel Warburton
FREE WILL Thomas Pink
FREEMASONRY Andreas Önnerfors
FRENCH LITERATURE John D. Lyons
FRENCH PHILOSOPHY Stephen Gaukroger and Knox Peden
THE FRENCH REVOLUTION William Doyle
FREUD Anthony Storr
FUNDAMENTALISM Malise Ruthven
FUNGI Nicholas P. Money
THE FUTURE Jennifer M. Gidley
GALAXIES John Gribbin
GALILEO Stillman Drake
GAME THEORY Ken Binmore
GANDHI Bhikhu Parekh
GARDEN HISTORY Gordon Campbell
GENES Jonathan Slack
GENIUS Andrew Robinson
GENOMICS John Archibald
GEOGRAPHY John Matthews and David Herbert
GEOLOGY Jan Zalasiewicz
GEOMETRY Maciej Dunajski
GEOPHYSICS William Lowrie
GEOPOLITICS Klaus Dodds
GERMAN LITERATURE Nicholas Boyle
GERMAN PHILOSOPHY Andrew Bowie
THE GHETTO Bryan Cheyette
GLACIATION David J. A. Evans
GLOBAL CATASTROPHES Bill McGuire
GLOBAL ECONOMIC HISTORY Robert C. Allen
GLOBAL ISLAM Nile Green
GLOBALIZATION Manfred B. Steger
GOD John Bowker
GÖDEL'S THEOREM A. W. Moore
GOETHE Ritchie Robertson
THE GOTHIC Nick Groom
GOVERNANCE Mark Bevir
GRAVITY Timothy Clifton
THE GREAT DEPRESSION AND THE NEW DEAL Eric Rauchway
HABEAS CORPUS Amanda Tyler
HABERMAS James Gordon Finlayson
THE HABSBURG EMPIRE Martyn Rady
HAPPINESS Daniel M. Haybron
THE HARLEM RENAISSANCE Cheryl A. Wall
THE HEBREW BIBLE AS LITERATURE Tod Linafelt
HEGEL Peter Singer
HEIDEGGER Michael Inwood
THE HELLENISTIC AGE Peter Thonemann
HEREDITY John Waller
HERMENEUTICS Jens Zimmermann
HERODOTUS Jennifer T. Roberts
HIEROGLYPHS Penelope Wilson
HINDUISM Kim Knott
HISTORY John H. Arnold
THE HISTORY OF ASTRONOMY Michael Hoskin
THE HISTORY OF CHEMISTRY William H. Brock
THE HISTORY OF CHILDHOOD James Marten
THE HISTORY OF CINEMA Geoffrey Nowell-Smith
THE HISTORY OF COMPUTING Doron Swade
THE HISTORY OF LIFE Michael Benton
THE HISTORY OF MATHEMATICS Jacqueline Stedall
THE HISTORY OF MEDICINE William Bynum
THE HISTORY OF PHYSICS J. L. Heilbron
THE HISTORY OF POLITICAL THOUGHT Richard Whatmore
THE HISTORY OF TIME Leofranc Holford-Strevens
HIV AND AIDS Alan Whiteside
HOBBES Richard Tuck
HOLLYWOOD Peter Decherney
THE HOLY ROMAN EMPIRE Joachim Whaley
HOME Michael Allen Fox
HOMER Barbara Graziosi
HORMONES Martin Luck
HORROR Darryl Jones
HUMAN ANATOMY Leslie Klenerman
HUMAN EVOLUTION Bernard Wood
HUMAN PHYSIOLOGY Jamie A. Davies

HUMAN RESOURCE MANAGEMENT Adrian Wilkinson
HUMAN RIGHTS Andrew Clapham
HUMANISM Stephen Law
HUME James A. Harris
HUMOUR Noël Carroll
THE ICE AGE Jamie Woodward
IDENTITY Florian Coulmas
IDEOLOGY Michael Freeden
THE IMMUNE SYSTEM Paul Klenerman
INDIAN CINEMA Ashish Rajadhyaksha
INDIAN PHILOSOPHY Sue Hamilton
THE INDUSTRIAL REVOLUTION Robert C. Allen
INFECTIOUS DISEASE Marta L. Wayne and Benjamin M. Bolker
INFINITY Ian Stewart
INFORMATION Luciano Floridi
INNOVATION Mark Dodgson and David Gann
INTELLECTUAL PROPERTY Siva Vaidhyanathan
INTELLIGENCE Ian J. Deary
INTERNATIONAL LAW Vaughan Lowe
INTERNATIONAL MIGRATION Khalid Koser
INTERNATIONAL RELATIONS Christian Reus-Smit
INTERNATIONAL SECURITY Christopher S. Browning
INSECTS Simon Leather
IRAN Ali M. Ansari
ISLAM Malise Ruthven
ISLAMIC HISTORY Adam Silverstein
ISLAMIC LAW Mashood A. Baderin
ISOTOPES Rob Ellam
ITALIAN LITERATURE Peter Hainsworth and David Robey
HENRY JAMES Susan L. Mizruchi
JESUS Richard Bauckham
JEWISH HISTORY David N. Myers
JEWISH LITERATURE Ilan Stavans
JOURNALISM Ian Hargreaves
JAMES JOYCE Colin MacCabe
JUDAISM Norman Solomon
JUNG Anthony Stevens
KABBALAH Joseph Dan
KAFKA Ritchie Robertson
KANT Roger Scruton
KEYNES Robert Skidelsky
KIERKEGAARD Patrick Gardiner
KNOWLEDGE Jennifer Nagel
THE KORAN Michael Cook
KOREA Michael J. Seth
LAKES Warwick F. Vincent
LANDSCAPE ARCHITECTURE Ian H. Thompson
LANDSCAPES AND GEOMORPHOLOGY Andrew Goudie and Heather Viles
LANGUAGES Stephen R. Anderson
LATE ANTIQUITY Gillian Clark
LAW Raymond Wacks
THE LAWS OF THERMODYNAMICS Peter Atkins
LEADERSHIP Keith Grint
LEARNING Mark Haselgrove
LEIBNIZ Maria Rosa Antognazza
C. S. LEWIS James Como
LIBERALISM Michael Freeden
LIGHT Ian Walmsley
LINCOLN Allen C. Guelzo
LINGUISTICS Peter Matthews
LITERARY THEORY Jonathan Culler
LOCKE John Dunn
LOGIC Graham Priest
LOVE Ronald de Sousa
MARTIN LUTHER Scott H. Hendrix
MACHIAVELLI Quentin Skinner
MADNESS Andrew Scull
MAGIC Owen Davies
MAGNA CARTA Nicholas Vincent
MAGNETISM Stephen Blundell
MALTHUS Donald Winch
MAMMALS T. S. Kemp
MANAGEMENT John Hendry
NELSON MANDELA Elleke Boehmer
MAO Delia Davin
MARINE BIOLOGY Philip V. Mladenov
MARKETING Kenneth Le Meunier-FitzHugh
THE MARQUIS DE SADE John Phillips
MARTYRDOM Jolyon Mitchell
MARX Peter Singer
MATERIALS Christopher Hall
MATHEMATICAL FINANCE Mark H. A. Davis
MATHEMATICS Timothy Gowers
MATTER Geoff Cottrell

THE MAYA Matthew Restall and Amara Solari
THE MEANING OF LIFE Terry Eagleton
MEASUREMENT David Hand
MEDICAL ETHICS Michael Dunn and Tony Hope
MEDICAL LAW Charles Foster
MEDIEVAL BRITAIN John Gillingham and Ralph A. Griffiths
MEDIEVAL LITERATURE Elaine Treharne
MEDIEVAL PHILOSOPHY John Marenbon
MEMORY Jonathan K. Foster
METAPHYSICS Stephen Mumford
METHODISM William J. Abraham
THE MEXICAN REVOLUTION Alan Knight
MICROBIOLOGY Nicholas P. Money
MICROECONOMICS Avinash Dixit
MICROSCOPY Terence Allen
THE MIDDLE AGES Miri Rubin
MILITARY JUSTICE Eugene R. Fidell
MILITARY STRATEGY Antulio J. Echevarria II
JOHN STUART MILL Gregory Claeys
MINERALS David Vaughan
MIRACLES Yujin Nagasawa
MODERN ARCHITECTURE Adam Sharr
MODERN ART David Cottington
MODERN BRAZIL Anthony W. Pereira
MODERN CHINA Rana Mitter
MODERN DRAMA Kirsten E. Shepherd-Barr
MODERN FRANCE Vanessa R. Schwartz
MODERN INDIA Craig Jeffrey
MODERN IRELAND Senia Pašeta
MODERN ITALY Anna Cento Bull
MODERN JAPAN Christopher Goto-Jones
MODERN LATIN AMERICAN LITERATURE Roberto González Echevarría
MODERN WAR Richard English
MODERNISM Christopher Butler
MOLECULAR BIOLOGY Aysha Divan and Janice A. Royds
MOLECULES Philip Ball
MONASTICISM Stephen J. Davis
THE MONGOLS Morris Rossabi
MONTAIGNE William M. Hamlin
MOONS David A. Rothery
MORMONISM Richard Lyman Bushman
MOUNTAINS Martin F. Price
MUHAMMAD Jonathan A. C. Brown
MULTICULTURALISM Ali Rattansi
MULTILINGUALISM John C. Maher
MUSIC Nicholas Cook
MUSIC AND TECHNOLOGY Mark Katz
MYTH Robert A. Segal
NAPOLEON David Bell
THE NAPOLEONIC WARS Mike Rapport
NATIONALISM Steven Grosby
NATIVE AMERICAN LITERATURE Sean Teuton
NAVIGATION Jim Bennett
NAZI GERMANY Jane Caplan
NEGOTIATION Carrie Menkel-Meadow
NEOLIBERALISM Manfred B. Steger and Ravi K. Roy
NETWORKS Guido Caldarelli and Michele Catanzaro
THE NEW TESTAMENT Luke Timothy Johnson
THE NEW TESTAMENT AS LITERATURE Kyle Keefer
NEWTON Robert Iliffe
NIETZSCHE Michael Tanner
NINETEENTH-CENTURY BRITAIN Christopher Harvie and H. C. G. Matthew
THE NORMAN CONQUEST George Garnett
NORTH AMERICAN INDIANS Theda Perdue and Michael D. Green
NORTHERN IRELAND Marc Mulholland
NOTHING Frank Close
NUCLEAR PHYSICS Frank Close
NUCLEAR POWER Maxwell Irvine
NUCLEAR WEAPONS Joseph M. Siracusa
NUMBER THEORY Robin Wilson
NUMBERS Peter M. Higgins

NUTRITION David A. Bender
OBJECTIVITY Stephen Gaukroger
OCEANS Dorrik Stow
THE OLD TESTAMENT Michael D. Coogan
THE ORCHESTRA D. Kern Holoman
ORGANIC CHEMISTRY Graham Patrick
ORGANIZATIONS Mary Jo Hatch
ORGANIZED CRIME Georgios A. Antonopoulos and Georgios Papanicolaou
ORTHODOX CHRISTIANITY A. Edward Siecienski
OVID Llewelyn Morgan
PAGANISM Owen Davies
PAKISTAN Pippa Virdee
THE PALESTINIAN-ISRAELI CONFLICT Martin Bunton
PANDEMICS Christian W. McMillen
PARTICLE PHYSICS Frank Close
PAUL E. P. Sanders
IVAN PAVLOV Daniel P. Todes
PEACE Oliver P. Richmond
PENTECOSTALISM William K. Kay
PERCEPTION Brian Rogers
THE PERIODIC TABLE Eric R. Scerri
PHILOSOPHICAL METHOD Timothy Williamson
PHILOSOPHY Edward Craig
PHILOSOPHY IN THE ISLAMIC WORLD Peter Adamson
PHILOSOPHY OF BIOLOGY Samir Okasha
PHILOSOPHY OF LAW Raymond Wacks
PHILOSOPHY OF MIND Barbara Gail Montero
PHILOSOPHY OF PHYSICS David Wallace
PHILOSOPHY OF SCIENCE Samir Okasha
PHILOSOPHY OF RELIGION Tim Bayne
PHOTOGRAPHY Steve Edwards
PHYSICAL CHEMISTRY Peter Atkins
PHYSICS Sidney Perkowitz
PILGRIMAGE Ian Reader
PLAGUE Paul Slack
PLANETARY SYSTEMS Raymond T. Pierrehumbert
PLANETS David A. Rothery
PLANTS Timothy Walker
PLATE TECTONICS Peter Molnar
PLATO Julia Annas
POETRY Bernard O'Donoghue
POLITICAL PHILOSOPHY David Miller
POLITICS Kenneth Minogue
POLYGAMY Sarah M. S. Pearsall
POPULISM Cas Mudde and Cristóbal Rovira Kaltwasser
POSTCOLONIALISM Robert Young
POSTMODERNISM Christopher Butler
POSTSTRUCTURALISM Catherine Belsey
POVERTY Philip N. Jefferson
PREHISTORY Chris Gosden
PRESOCRATIC PHILOSOPHY Catherine Osborne
PRIVACY Raymond Wacks
PROBABILITY John Haigh
PROGRESSIVISM Walter Nugent
PROHIBITION W. J. Rorabaugh
PROJECTS Andrew Davies
PROTESTANTISM Mark A. Noll
PSYCHIATRY Tom Burns
PSYCHOANALYSIS Daniel Pick
PSYCHOLOGY Gillian Butler and Freda McManus
PSYCHOLOGY OF MUSIC Elizabeth Hellmuth Margulis
PSYCHOPATHY Essi Viding
PSYCHOTHERAPY Tom Burns and Eva Burns-Lundgren
PUBLIC ADMINISTRATION Stella Z. Theodoulou and Ravi K. Roy
PUBLIC HEALTH Virginia Berridge
PURITANISM Francis J. Bremer
THE QUAKERS Pink Dandelion
QUANTUM THEORY John Polkinghorne
RACISM Ali Rattansi
RADIOACTIVITY Claudio Tuniz
RASTAFARI Ennis B. Edmonds
READING Belinda Jack
THE REAGAN REVOLUTION Gil Troy
REALITY Jan Westerhoff
RECONSTRUCTION Allen C. Guelzo
THE REFORMATION Peter Marshall

REFUGEES Gil Loescher
RELATIVITY Russell Stannard
RELIGION Thomas A. Tweed
RELIGION IN AMERICA Timothy Beal
THE RENAISSANCE Jerry Brotton
RENAISSANCE ART
Geraldine A. Johnson
RENEWABLE ENERGY Nick Jelley
REPTILES T. S. Kemp
REVOLUTIONS Jack A. Goldstone
RHETORIC Richard Toye
RISK Baruch Fischhoff and John Kadvany
RITUAL Barry Stephenson
RIVERS Nick Middleton
ROBOTICS Alan Winfield
ROCKS Jan Zalasiewicz
ROMAN BRITAIN Peter Salway
THE ROMAN EMPIRE
Christopher Kelly
THE ROMAN REPUBLIC
David M. Gwynn
ROMANTICISM Michael Ferber
ROUSSEAU Robert Wokler
RUSSELL A. C. Grayling
THE RUSSIAN ECONOMY
Richard Connolly
RUSSIAN HISTORY Geoffrey Hosking
RUSSIAN LITERATURE Catriona Kelly
THE RUSSIAN REVOLUTION
S. A. Smith
SAINTS Simon Yarrow
SAMURAI Michael Wert
SAVANNAS Peter A. Furley
SCEPTICISM Duncan Pritchard
SCHIZOPHRENIA Chris Frith and
Eve Johnstone
SCHOPENHAUER
Christopher Janaway
SCIENCE AND RELIGION
Thomas Dixon and Adam R. Shapiro
SCIENCE FICTION David Seed
THE SCIENTIFIC REVOLUTION
Lawrence M. Principe
SCOTLAND Rab Houston
SECULARISM Andrew Copson
SEXUAL SELECTION Marlene Zuk and
Leigh W. Simmons
SEXUALITY Véronique Mottier
WILLIAM SHAKESPEARE Stanley Wells
SHAKESPEARE'S COMEDIES
Bart van Es
SHAKESPEARE'S SONNETS AND
POEMS Jonathan F. S. Post
SHAKESPEARE'S TRAGEDIES
Stanley Wells
GEORGE BERNARD SHAW
Christopher Wixson
MARY SHELLEY Charlotte Gordon
THE SHORT STORY Andrew Kahn
SIKHISM Eleanor Nesbitt
SILENT FILM Donna Kornhaber
THE SILK ROAD James A. Millward
SLANG Jonathon Green
SLEEP Steven W. Lockley and
Russell G. Foster
SMELL Matthew Cobb
ADAM SMITH Christopher J. Berry
SOCIAL AND CULTURAL
ANTHROPOLOGY
John Monaghan and Peter Just
SOCIAL PSYCHOLOGY Richard J. Crisp
SOCIAL WORK Sally Holland and
Jonathan Scourfield
SOCIALISM Michael Newman
SOCIOLINGUISTICS John Edwards
SOCIOLOGY Steve Bruce
SOCRATES C. C. W. Taylor
SOFT MATTER Tom McLeish
SOUND Mike Goldsmith
SOUTHEAST ASIA James R. Rush
THE SOVIET UNION Stephen Lovell
THE SPANISH CIVIL WAR
Helen Graham
SPANISH LITERATURE Jo Labanyi
THE SPARTANS Andrew Bayliss
SPINOZA Roger Scruton
SPIRITUALITY Philip Sheldrake
SPORT Mike Cronin
STARS Andrew King
STATISTICS David J. Hand
STEM CELLS Jonathan Slack
STOICISM Brad Inwood
STRUCTURAL ENGINEERING
David Blockley
STUART BRITAIN John Morrill
THE SUN Philip Judge
SUPERCONDUCTIVITY
Stephen Blundell
SUPERSTITION Stuart Vyse
SYMMETRY Ian Stewart
SYNAESTHESIA Julia Simner
SYNTHETIC BIOLOGY Jamie A. Davies

SYSTEMS BIOLOGY Eberhard O. Voit
TAXATION Stephen Smith
TEETH Peter S. Ungar
TELESCOPES Geoff Cottrell
TERRORISM Charles Townshend
THEATRE Marvin Carlson
THEOLOGY David F. Ford
THINKING AND REASONING Jonathan St B. T. Evans
THOUGHT Tim Bayne
TIBETAN BUDDHISM Matthew T. Kapstein
TIDES David George Bowers and Emyr Martyn Roberts
TIME Jenann Ismael
TOCQUEVILLE Harvey C. Mansfield
LEO TOLSTOY Liza Knapp
TOPOLOGY Richard Earl
TRAGEDY Adrian Poole
TRANSLATION Matthew Reynolds
THE TREATY OF VERSAILLES Michael S. Neiberg
TRIGONOMETRY Glen Van Brummelen
THE TROJAN WAR Eric H. Cline
TRUST Katherine Hawley
THE TUDORS John Guy
TWENTIETH-CENTURY BRITAIN Kenneth O. Morgan
TYPOGRAPHY Paul Luna
THE UNITED NATIONS Jussi M. Hanhimäki
UNIVERSITIES AND COLLEGES David Palfreyman and Paul Temple
THE U.S. CIVIL WAR Louis P. Masur
THE U.S. CONGRESS Donald A. Ritchie
THE U.S. CONSTITUTION David J. Bodenhamer
THE U.S. SUPREME COURT Linda Greenhouse
UTILITARIANISM Katarzyna de Lazari-Radek and Peter Singer
UTOPIANISM Lyman Tower Sargent
VETERINARY SCIENCE James Yeates
THE VIKINGS Julian D. Richards
VIOLENCE Philip Dwyer
THE VIRGIN MARY Mary Joan Winn Leith
THE VIRTUES Craig A. Boyd and Kevin Timpe
VIRUSES Dorothy H. Crawford
VOLCANOES Michael J. Branney and Jan Zalasiewicz
VOLTAIRE Nicholas Cronk
WAR AND RELIGION Jolyon Mitchell and Joshua Rey
WAR AND TECHNOLOGY Alex Roland
WATER John Finney
WAVES Mike Goldsmith
WEATHER Storm Dunlop
THE WELFARE STATE David Garland
WITCHCRAFT Malcolm Gaskill
WITTGENSTEIN A. C. Grayling
WORK Stephen Fineman
WORLD MUSIC Philip Bohlman
WORLD MYTHOLOGY David Leeming
THE WORLD TRADE ORGANIZATION Amrita Narlikar
WORLD WAR II Gerhard L. Weinberg
WRITING AND SCRIPT Andrew Robinson
ZIONISM Michael Stanislawski
ÉMILE ZOLA Brian Nelson

Available soon:

MICROBIOMES Angela E. Douglas
ANSELM Thomas Williams
ANCIENT GREEK AND ROMAN SCIENCE Liba Taub
ADDICTION Keith Humphreys
VATICAN II Shaun Blanchard & Stephen Bullivant
OBSERVATIONAL ASTRONOMY Geoff Cottrell
MATHEMATICAL ANALYSIS Richard Earl

Dana Villa

HANNAH ARENDT

A Very Short Introduction

OXFORD
UNIVERSITY PRESS

Great Clarendon Street, Oxford, OX2 6DP,
United Kingdom

Oxford University Press is a department of the University of Oxford.
It furthers the University's objective of excellence in research, scholarship,
and education by publishing worldwide. Oxford is a registered trade mark of
Oxford University Press in the UK and in certain other countries

First Edition published in 2023

Published in the United States of America by Oxford University Press
198 Madison Avenue, New York, NY 10016, United States of America

British Library Cataloguing in Publication Data
Data available

Library of Congress Control Number: 2022935029

ISBN 978-0-19-880698-1

Printed and bound by
CPI Group (UK) Ltd, Croydon, CR0 4YY

Contents

Acknowledgments

I would like to thank George Kateb for encouraging my interest in Hannah Arendt many years ago. I would also like to thank Katy Arnold for reading chapter drafts and offering suggestions.

List of illustrations

List of abbreviations

BPF	Hannah Arendt, *Between Past and Future*
CAJ	Hannah Arendt, Karl Jaspers, *Correspondence: 1926–1969*
CCA	*The Cambridge Companion to Hannah Arendt*, ed. Dana Villa
CJ	Immanuel Kant, *Critique of Judgment*
EJ	Hannah Arendt, *Eichmann in Jerusalem*
LKPP	Hannah Arendt, *Lectures on Kant's Political Philosophy*
LM	Hannah Arendt, *The Life of the Mind*
MC	Margaret Canovan, *Hannah Arendt: A Reinterpretation of her Political Thought*
MDT	Hannah Arendt, *Men in Dark Times*
OR	Hannah Arendt, *On Revolution*
OT	Hannah Arendt, *The Origins of Totalitarianism*
THC	Hannah Arendt, *The Human Condition*
TMC	Hannah Arendt, "Thinking and Moral Considerations," in Arendt, *Responsibility and Judgment*
TWB	Hannah Arendt, *Thinking Without a Bannister*
YB	Elisabeth Young-Bruehl, *Hannah Arendt: For Love of the World*

Chapter 1
A life in dark times

Hannah Arendt was born on October 14, 1906, in Hanover, Germany (Figure 1). Shortly after her birth, her parents, Paul and Martha Arendt, moved to Königsberg, the provincial capital of East Prussia. Famous as the hometown of Enlightenment philosopher Immanuel Kant, Königsberg was a port city with a substantial Jewish population (about 5,000). Most of Königsberg's Jews came from Russia or Lithuania. Hannah Arendt's great-grandfather on her maternal side (the Cohns) was a Lithuanian trader and subject of the Russian Empire. Faced with the prospect of conscription into the tsar's army in 1851, he promptly fled across the border to Königsberg, where he set up what became a successful tea exporting business, J. N. Cohn and Company (YB, 6). Hannah Arendt described her father's family, the Arendts, as an "old Königsberg family" whose German identity was hardly doubted.

Arendt's childhood was marked by the early death of her father, who had contracted syphilis as a young man and never received adequate medical treatment. Arendt witnessed her father's slow and terrifying decline over a period of three years. When he finally died in 1913, the 7-year-old Hannah became her mother's primary consoler (YB, 20). She herself did not display great grief at the time of her father's death, but she was often ill and secluded at home during her early school years. The full impact of her father's

1. Hannah Arendt with her mother at the age of 8 (1914).

death came later, and depression almost overtook her during her university years.

With the outbreak of World War I, the Russian army advanced on Königsberg. Arendt and her mother retreated to Berlin to stay with relatives. They returned to Königsberg 10 weeks later once the Russian advance was halted by the German army. The Cohn family fortune provided for them during the worst years of the war, but by 1918 the family business had begun to fail.

At the end of World War I revolution broke out in Berlin and Munich. The Spartacists, a radical left-wing group led by Rosa Luxemburg and Karl Liebknecht, successfully called for a general strike. For a moment they seemed in sight of their goal of establishing a socialist republic. However, both Luxemburg and Liebknecht were murdered by right-wing *Freikorps* paramilitaries, and the short-lived Bavarian Räterepublik (council republic) was put down by counter-revolutionary forces. Throughout her life Arendt would remember her mother's excitement during those revolutionary weeks. Luxemburg's idea of a "spontaneous" revolution, one led by self-organized workers' and soldiers' councils, made a permanent impression on her.

A year after the revolution, Arendt's mother remarried. Martin Beerwald was the son of a Jewish moneylender, a widower, and the father of two daughters, Eva and Clara. Hannah now had two stepsisters, whom she followed into the Luiseschule, the *Gymnasium* for girls in Königsberg. She had previously established an intellectually stimulating circle of older peers, drawn mainly from sons and daughters of her mother's friends. Many of them were university students, and they brought back stories of their most intellectually adventurous professors, including the still largely unknown Martin Heidegger at Marburg.

Hannah Arendt excelled academically in the Luiseschule but displayed an independent streak that did not endear her to her teachers. At the age of 15, she responded to an instructor's rude remark by organizing a student boycott of his classes. The school authorities did not look kindly on such behavior, and she was expelled. Determined that her daughter continue her education, Martha Arendt arranged for Hannah to spend several semesters at the University of Berlin. While there she studied Greek and Latin, and also attended lectures on Christian theology by Romano Guardini, a well-known Christian existentialist. Thus fortified, she was able to take the all-important *Abitur* (graduation exam) at the Luiseschule as an "extraneous scholar." With success in the examination and her *Gymnasium* degree, she was ready to become a real university student. In 1924 she elected to go to Marburg.

In the period 1924–6, when Arendt was his student, Heidegger taught courses on Aristotle's *Rhetoric* and Plato's *Sophist*. Arendt was exposed not only to Heidegger's radical revision of the phenomenological method he had learned from Edmund Husserl, but also to his approach to the texts of the past. Heidegger's "destructive" approach emphasized the need to break through the husks of traditional interpretations, the better to engage Plato, Aristotle, Kant, et al. in a living philosophical dialogue. In contrast to Heidegger's acolytes, Arendt never mimicked his difficult style or esoteric language. She did, however, imbibe his general approach. Like Heidegger, Arendt was a "pearl diver" who descended "to the bottom of the sea" (meaning, in the case of the Western tradition of philosophical thought, the ancient Greeks) "not to excavate the bottom and bring it to light but to pry loose the rich and the strange." These "thought fragments" could, once recovered, be made to speak in the present (*MDT*, 205–6).

That the 35-year-old Heidegger was charismatic in the eyes of the "resolute starvelings" studying philosophy during these years is beyond doubt. The 18-year-old Arendt was attracted to him romantically. During her time at Marburg, she and the married Heidegger had an affair. Retrospectively, Arendt viewed her relationship with Heidegger as the first great passion of her life, and Heidegger would later claim that Arendt was his philosophical muse during these years. Nevertheless, it was clear to them both that Arendt would have to finish her degree with someone else. In 1926 she left Marburg, first for Freiburg, then on to Heidelberg to study with Heidegger's friend and fellow *Existenzphilosophe*, Karl Jaspers. It was with Jaspers that Arendt wrote her doctoral dissertation, "The Concept of Love in St. Augustine."

Her doctoral work complete, Arendt moved from Heidelberg to Berlin in 1929—the year of the stock market crash in New York and the beginning of the Great Depression. The Weimar Republic's shaky foundations became even shakier with mounting unemployment and the advent of hyper-inflation. While in Heidelberg Arendt continued to see Heidegger, but his attraction to the idea of a conservative revolution, one led by the Nazi party, effectively put an end to all contact between them for 17 years.

Attending a fund-raising event for a small Marxist journal in Berlin, Arendt ran into a young Jewish philosophy student, Gunther Stern. Arendt had met Stern previously in Heidelberg but had shown little interest. This time her response was decidedly different and they were soon living together. Stern had decided to write a *Habilitationschrift*, the second dissertation required for academic employment as a lecturer (or *Privatdozent*) at a German university. His chosen subject was the philosophy of music, and—after receiving encouragement from the faculty at Frankfurt—he and Arendt moved there.

Arendt and Stern married prior to relocating to Frankfurt. However, Stern's quest for academic accreditation soon ran into a brick wall in the form of Theodor Adorno, who had his own ideas about the philosophy of music. After two years of frustration, the Sterns returned to Berlin and Gunther reinvented himself as the journalist "Gunther Anders."

Upon returning to Berlin Arendt renewed her acquaintance with Kurt Blumenfeld. Blumenfeld was a Zionist who had been a student in Königsberg during Arendt's childhood, and he had often argued with Arendt's grandfather about the place of Jews in German society. In Berlin, he welcomed Arendt into his circle of fellow Zionists, and their discussions raised Arendt's political consciousness while giving her a fuller sense of her German-Jewish identity.

By 1932 Arendt and Stern were moving in distinctly different circles. Stern's circle consisted of artists, journalists, and intellectuals in and around the German Communist Party, while Arendt's consisted mainly of Zionists like Blumenfeld. Arendt and her husband were clearly drifting apart. After the Reichstag fire (February 1933) Stern suddenly found himself in great danger. The Gestapo, having confiscated Bertolt Brecht's address book, were using it to round up Communist Party members and their associates. Stern fled to Paris, while Arendt stayed in Berlin (Figure 2).

The occasion for Arendt's own escape from Germany came when Blumenfeld asked her to collect materials from the Prussian State Library revealing anti-Semitic policies and actions in German business and professional associations. The idea was to use these to inform the world about the increasingly tenuous situation faced by Jews in Germany.

Since Blumenfeld and his associates were all members of the German Zionist Organization, the arrest of any one of them would have put the entire membership at risk. Arendt was not a member and could therefore undertake the mission without endangering the group. She accepted the assignment, but was discovered and arrested while carrying it out. The arresting officer, who had only recently transferred to the political department, had little idea of what he was supposed to do with someone like Arendt. Sympathetic to the plight of Jews, he promised to get her released. Eight days later she was free. After an evening spent celebrating

2. Hannah Arendt in 1933.

with Blumenfeld, Arendt and her mother made use of an "underground railway" that was shepherding Jews and leftists out of Germany. With their help, the two were able to cross over the border into Czechoslovakia. Hannah Arendt began what was to be 18 years as a stateless person.

From Prague Arendt went to Geneva, and then on to Paris, where she reunited with Stern. She was able to secure a job at Agriculture et Artisanat, an agency that gave young Jewish émigrés training in farming and crafts to prepare them for emigration to Palestine. Some months later she began working with Youth Aliyah, a Jewish organization with a similar mission.

By 1936, a group of German Jewish intellectuals and artists including the critic Walter Benjamin had replaced Blumenfeld and his Berlin friends as Arendt's chief interlocutors. Many in this group had Marxist backgrounds. Among them was the former Spartacist Heinrich Blücher. Like Arendt, Blücher had fled from Berlin to Paris via Prague. An autodidact, he had immersed himself in the writings of Marx and Trotsky. At the time of their meeting in Paris, both Blücher and Arendt were estranged from their spouses. They fell in love, moved in together, procured divorces, and (ultimately) married in January 1940.

In 1938 the Paris office of Youth Aliyah relocated to London. Arendt stayed in Paris and began working for the Jewish Agency, an organization which aided Austrian and Czechoslovakian refugees in France. Soon after *Kristallnacht* (November 8, 1938), Arendt's mother—who had returned to Germany to live with her second husband in Königsberg—left Germany for good and joined her daughter and Blücher in Paris. The Nazi invasion of Poland commenced on September 1, 1939, leading France and Great Britain to declare war on Germany on September 3.

At the beginning of May 1940, the Governor-General of Paris ordered all refugees from Germany to report for transport to

French internment camps. Arendt and her mother wound up in a camp for "enemy alien" women at Gurs, while Blücher found himself interned at a camp for men at Villemalard. The quick defeat of France at the end of June threw the camps into a state of confusion. Arendt and her mother seized the opportunity to escape to Montauban where, miraculously, Arendt ran into Blücher on the street.

Montauban was in Vichy France. In October 1940 the regime ordered all Jews to register with local prefects of police. Sensing what might lie ahead, Arendt applied for an exit visa. The Blüchers' plan was to leave Europe and emigrate to America, even though the US government at this point was hardly welcoming to European refugees. Thanks to her position in Youth Aliyah, however, Arendt was granted special consideration. She was able to obtain a visa for herself and her husband (Martha Arendt's visa was processed later). Making their way to Marseilles, the Blüchers reunited with their friend Walter Benjamin.

The Vichy government's reluctance to issue exit permits meant that Jewish refugees, even those with visas, wound up stuck in Marseilles, uncertain whether they would ever get out. Fortunately for Arendt and Blücher the government briefly relaxed its policy, and in January 1941 they were able to board a train to Lisbon. Benjamin stayed behind. He met with a tragic end when his attempt to cross over the Franco-Spanish border at Port Bou was frustrated by border guards on the Spanish side. The guards had unexpectedly closed the border, and Benjamin, despairing, committed suicide by taking an overdose of morphine. The next day, the border reopened.

Perhaps sensing his fate, Benjamin had entrusted Arendt with some of his manuscripts, including the famous "Theses on the Philosophy of History." These were among the Blüchers' belongings when they set sail from Lisbon to America in May 1941.

The Blüchers arrived in New York City the same month, renting two small rooms on W. 95th Street. Arendt delivered the suitcase containing Benjamin's manuscripts to Adorno at the offices of the Institute for Social Research, which had set up headquarters-in-exile at Columbia University. Since neither of the Blüchers knew English, Arendt took advantage of a program offered by Self-Help for Refugees and traveled to Winchester, Massachusetts to spend two months as the guest of an American family.

Back in New York, Arendt visited Salo Baron, a scholar of Jewish history, at Columbia. With his encouragement, she submitted an essay titled "From the Dreyfus Affair to France Today," which Baron published in *Jewish Social Studies*. He thus provided Arendt with a crucial credential for the American academy. However, her desire at the time was to do work of a more political nature. After hearing Blumenfeld present a lecture at the German-Jewish Club of New York on whether there should be a Jewish Army in the struggle against Hitler, Arendt wrote an article titled "The Jewish Army—the Beginning of a Jewish Politics?" This was published in *Aufbau*, the club's newsletter.

The essay argued for the formation of a Jewish army to fight alongside the allies in Europe. Not only would such an army help defend the Jewish people, it would also provide a vitally needed political identity (YB, 171). Arendt's critical stance toward the Zionist position (they saw the British restriction of Jewish emigration to Palestine, not the war in Europe, as the primary issue) established her intellectual independence, but it did so at the price of practical-political influence. Martha Arendt had, by this time, joined the Blüchers in New York, taking a room right above the two small ones inhabited by Arendt and her husband. In these straitened circumstances Arendt began planning *The Origins of Totalitarianism.*

During her years of work on *Origins* Arendt was employed first as a researcher for the Commission on European Jewish Cultural

Reconstruction (1944–6), and later as an executive director of its successor organization, Jewish Cultural Reconstruction (1948–52). As researcher she drew up a "Tentative List of Jewish Cultural Treasures in Axis-Occupied Countries," which was published in *Jewish Social Studies*. In her capacity as executive director she oversaw the effort to recover as many of these treasures as possible, traveling to Europe herself for six months in 1949–50.

The great success of *The Origins of Totalitarianism* lifted Arendt out of semi-obscurity and made her internationally famous. Despite its positive reception, reviewers of the book pointed out the imbalance between Arendt's analysis of the nature and sources of National Socialism and her less thorough analysis of the nature and sources of Bolshevism. In part this was a function of the relative inaccessibility of archival material from the Soviet Union. But it was also because Bolshevik ideology, unlike Nazism, could lay claim to a respectable intellectual genealogy, emerging as it did out of the work of Karl Marx.

When she wrote *Origins* Arendt was aware of this imbalance, as well as her failure to come to grips with Bolshevism's appropriation of the Marxian legacy. This led her to apply to the Guggenheim Foundation for a grant to work on a book about the "totalitarian elements in Marxism." Originally projected to be a relatively short work, the manuscript was left unfinished.

What prevented Arendt from completing the Marx project as planned? The short answer is that the more deeply she read in Marx, the more conscious she became of the fact that he stood on the other side of the "break in the tradition" effected by the emergence of totalitarianism in Europe. The unprecedented policies of genocide, mass murder, and rule by terror characteristic of this "novel form of government" shattered any illusion of continuity with the Western tradition of philosophical and political thought. The fact that Marx stood on the other side of the abyss opened by the advent of totalitarian domination made him, in many respects, far closer to the "lost" tradition than to the reality of Stalinism. Thus, when Arendt was invited to give the Gauss Seminars in Criticism at Princeton University in 1953, she set herself the task of showing how "the line from Aristotle to Marx shows both fewer and far less decisive breaks than the line from Marx to Stalin" (*TWB*, 6).

Arendt developed themes introduced in her Gauss lectures in a series of books: *The Human Condition* (1958), *Between Past and Future* (1961), and *On Revolution* (1963). Marx appears in all three, but only as one figure in a tradition of political philosophy that Arendt had come to view as inherently hostile to politics. One benefit of the "break in the tradition" was that it made a fresh examination of key political phenomena (such as human plurality, action, freedom, and opinion) possible, an examination unburdened by what Arendt saw as the philosophical tradition's anti-political prejudices.

In May of 1960, Israeli agents captured SS Lt. Colonel Adolf Eichmann in Buenos Aires, Argentina, where he had been living under the assumed name of Ricardo Klement. Ignoring Argentinian sovereignty, they spirited him out of the country to stand trial in Israel. Eichmann had played a key role in the Nazis' "Final Solution," organizing the transport of millions of Jewish men, women, and children from Nazi-created ghettos in central and eastern Europe to the killing centers at Auschwitz-Birkenau and elsewhere. When Arendt heard of Eichmann's capture and the Israeli government's plan to try him in Jerusalem, she proposed herself as trial reporter to William Shawn, editor of *The New Yorker*. Shawn accepted, and Arendt traveled to Jerusalem to attend Eichmann's trial, which commenced on April 11, 1961.

Confronted by Eichmann in the flesh, Arendt was forced to abandon many of her preconceptions. Like others at the trial, she expected a vicious anti-Semite and an unregenerate SS man. Instead, what she encountered was an extremely ordinary individual, one whose key distinguishing characteristic was a truly remarkable degree of "thoughtlessness." By this Arendt meant not that Eichmann was stupid or mindless, but rather that he lacked the capacity to view things from another person's point of view or to engage in any independent thought or judgment of his own.

This is the origin of Arendt's famous notion of "the banality of evil." Arendt's suggestion that many entirely ordinary ("normal") people were to be found among the perpetrators of the most horrifying of crimes was initially found shocking, but is now widely accepted. At the time it was claimed that Arendt's "trial report" (published in book form as *Eichmann in Jerusalem* in 1963) somehow "exculpated" Eichmann by suggesting he wasn't exactly the "monster" many had presumed him to be. Many of Arendt's readers, particularly in the American Jewish community, found the idea of a "normal" Nazi hard to swallow. A bitter controversy ensued, with Arendt losing many friends—including her mentor Kurt Blumenfeld—in the process (Figure 3).

The 1960s was a tumultuous decade, and new debates—over civil rights, the American intervention in Vietnam, and the cause of Third World revolution—soon eclipsed the controversy that had erupted over the Eichmann book. Having answered her critics in the pages of *The New York Review of Books* and in the essay "Truth and Politics," Arendt expanded her role as one of America's most respected public intellectuals during these turbulent times. Worries about the uncritical endorsement of Third World revolution by the New Left led her to write "Reflections on Violence" (1969), while her approval of the anti-war movement found expression in the essay "Civil Disobedience" (1970).

In her last years, Arendt turned from political theory back to "philosophy proper" in her consideration of what she considered to be the mind's three most important faculties: thinking, willing, and judging. Her plan was to write a two-volume work, with

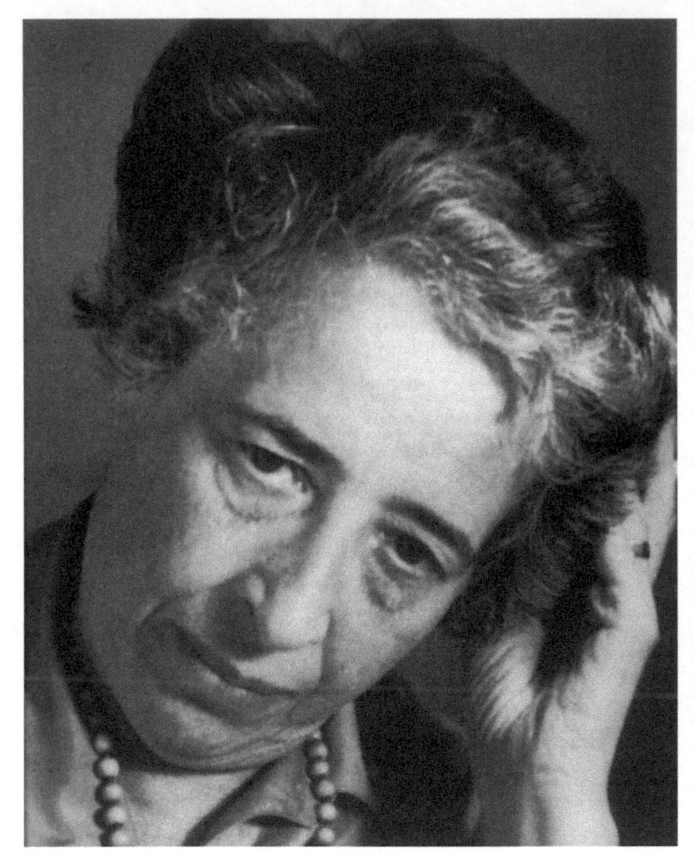

3. Hannah Arendt in 1963.

consideration of thinking as a mental activity constituting the first volume, and consideration of willing and judging the second.

In the spring of 1972 she received an invitation to give the Gifford Lectures at the University of Aberdeen. She gave the first set of lectures, on thinking, in spring of 1973. She returned to give the second set, on willing, in May 1974. In the middle of her first

"Willing" lecture, she suffered what turned out to be a near-fatal heart attack. After recuperating in Switzerland for the summer she returned to New York, where she continued teaching at the New School and planned for retirement.

In 1975 Arendt was awarded the Danish government's Sonning Prize for Contributions to European Civilization. She gave a memorable but highly critical address, "Home to Roost," at an American Bicentennial ceremony in Boston in May. She then traveled to the Deutsche Literaturarchiv in Marbach, Germany, where she sorted Karl Jaspers's correspondence (he had died in 1969). After an exhausting month, she visited the aging Heidegger for one last time.

Arendt returned to New York in September. The day after Thanksgiving, she fell as she walked from a taxi to the entrance of her building on Riverside Drive. She was able to get up and enter on her own and scheduled an appointment with her doctor. Bad weather gave her an excuse to cancel it. Ignorant of possible internal damage, Arendt hosted Salo Baron and his wife for dinner on December 4, 1975. After serving dessert, she sat down in her chair, coughed, and lost consciousness. To the Barons' shock, she was dead. After a memorial service in New York her ashes were buried next to those of Heinrich Blücher on the Bard College Campus, where Blücher had taught. At the time of her demise, Arendt had barely begun work on the "Judging" portion of *The Life of the Mind*. Her friend, the novelist Mary McCarthy, edited the volumes on thinking and willing and these were published, posthumously, in 1978.

Chapter 2
The nature and roots of totalitarianism

The Origins of Totalitarianism is a hard book to get a grip on. The reader is confronted by a long and difficult text, one which addresses a bewildering array of topics. The text's tripartite division into "Antisemitism," "Imperialism," and "Totalitarianism" is clear enough. However, Arendt's analyses of European Jewry's relationship to state and society; the imperialist ambitions of the bourgeoisie; the intellectual roots of European racism; the pan-German and pan-Slav movements; the internal contradictions of the nation-state as political form; the inter-war breakdown of the European class system; the distinctive nature of totalitarian movements; the unprecedented character of "total domination"; and (finally) the role of concentration camps within totalitarian regimes are likely to leave the reader baffled as to how all the pieces are supposed to fit together.

Part of the problem lies in the sheer scope and ambition of the task Arendt has set herself. In *OT* she is not attempting to give a historical account or sociological analysis of either Hitler's Germany or Stalin's Soviet Union (the presence of much historical and sociological analysis notwithstanding). Nor is she attempting to provide a causal *explanation* as to why and how totalitarianism as a regime form emerged in Europe and Russia between the wars. She is attempting, rather, to identify the critical *elements*—the practices, events, experiences, and attitudes—present in Europe between 1880 and 1933, elements whose combination made the emergence of something like totalitarianism possible.

I say "something like" because Arendt thought there was nothing predetermined about the appearance of totalitarianism in the heart of civilized Europe. The elements that made it possible appeared at a particular time and combined (or "crystallized") in a particular and unforeseeable way. Arendt never wants us to lose sight of the fact that the specific historical constellation created by these elements was *contingent*—as, indeed, was the event of totalitarian domination itself.

This is an important point, since theories of totalitarianism tend to deal in large historical-sociological abstractions such as "secularization," "atomization," "modernization," or "the development of monopoly capitalism." These are then made the linchpin of supposedly robust causal explanations. In marked contrast, Arendt thinks that the category of causal necessity has no legitimate place in the "historical sciences." Historical events are contingent: things could always have happened differently. A corollary of this is that there is no list of elements whose co-presence or combination creates totalitarianism as a predictable outcome. Nor is there any historical process that implicitly contains totalitarian domination as its ostensible *telos*.

In stressing this point, Arendt is combating not just the uncritical transfer of social science categories to historical-political analysis. She is also combating models of mechanistic causation we have inherited from the Enlightenment as well as teleological models of historical development we have inherited from 19th-century philosophies of history and social evolution (such as we find in Hegel, Marx, and Spencer). Unfortunately, both conceptions continue to inform "explanations" of totalitarianism. From Arendt's perspective, they impede rather than facilitate our attempt to *understand* what she considered to be a unique and unprecedented form of government.

For that, according to Arendt, is what totalitarianism was: a novel form of government, one that cannot be accounted for in terms of the traditional catalogue of regime forms (monarchy, aristocracy, democracy) and their respective "perversions" (tyranny, oligarchy, ochlocracy). If there is one central point Arendt wants her readers to take away from *OT*, it is that totalitarian regimes used organization and terror in new ways in order to achieve unprecedented ends. They wanted nothing less than to transform reality so that it would reflect their ideological fiction of a social world in constant evolutionary motion toward a predetermined end. For the Nazis, the grounding fiction was that of an inescapable "law of Nature" manifest in a biologically determined struggle of the races. For the Bolsheviks, the grounding fiction was that of an equally inescapable "law of History" manifest in an economically determined struggle of social classes.

To make messy and multi-dimensional reality reflect such undeniable "laws," the totalitarians undertook the project of shaping their citizen-subjects by means of political organization, propaganda, ideology, and terror. The goal was to create a populace neither motivated to, nor capable of, resisting such ostensibly all-determining forces. Achieving this goal depended upon the totalitarians' ability not only to eliminate substantial differences between individuals but also to effectively neutralize their capacity for spontaneous action and unpredictable behavior. Only when citizen-subjects were "stabilized" would it be possible for the shaping forces of Nature or History to move through the regime's "human material" in an accelerated and optimally efficient manner. In Arendt's view, the totalitarians came surprisingly close to achieving their goal of "changing human nature" so that it would accord with the deterministic demands of their ideologies.

The clearest indicator of this success is found in the concentration camps. It is hardly for rhetorical effect that Arendt labels them the "central institutions" of totalitarian regimes. It was in the camps that the elite groupings—the SS and the Bolshevik cadres—were trained to become ruthless executors of the "laws" of History or Nature, enslaving and liquidating those who belonged to "dying" classes or "inferior" races. Awareness of the camps' existence permeated the whole of totalitarian society, creating the fear that tomorrow could well be the day when one's ethnic, religious, professional, or class grouping would be added to the list of "objective" enemies of the regime. Such designation rendered entire categories of innocent people targets for liquidation.

However, the "real triumph of the system" is found in the transformation accomplished with respect to the camp prisoners themselves. Heads shaven, identified through numbers tattooed on their chests or arms, and clothed in filthy uniforms that offered no protection from the elements, the inmates of the lagers and the gulag were stripped of the remaining traces of their individuality and subjected to a regime of sustained and ruthlessly efficient dehumanization. Through forced labor, continual hunger, and the constant fear of beatings or shootings that required neither justification nor excuse, the prisoners in the camps were deprived not only of their rights and liberties but—ultimately—of their capacity to *act* or even behave in unpredictable ways, a capacity Arendt deems to be "distinctively human" (Figure 4).

The camps confront us starkly with the evil peculiar to totalitarian regimes, an evil that Arendt, adopting a phrase from Kant, calls "radical evil" (*OT*, 443). In a March 4, 1951 letter to her teacher and mentor Karl Jaspers she tries to explain what she means:

> What radical evil is I don't know, but it seems to me to do with the following phenomenon: making human beings as human beings superfluous (not using them as a means to an end, which leaves their essence as humans untouched and impinges only on their human dignity; rather, *making them superfluous as human beings*). This happens as soon as all unpredictability—which, in human beings is the equivalent of spontaneity—is eliminated. (*CAJ*, 166)

4. Slave laborers in the Buchenwald concentration camp, April 16, 1945.

It is the reduction of human beings to the status of expendable raw material that Arendt has in mind when she connects radical evil to "making human beings superfluous as human beings." Her point is that the totalitarians performed this reduction *not* out of "humanly understandable" motives such as selfishness, sadism, or cruelty. They performed it, rather, out of the hubristic conviction that *everything*—from remaking the world to changing human nature—*is possible* through the systematic employment of organization, propaganda, ideology, and terror. And they did it out of the deterministic conviction that their murderous programs constituted no more than the *acceleration* of an inescapable evolutionary process, the character and function of which had been previously laid down by the "laws" of Nature or History (*OT*, 427). Arendt sees this odd combination of hubris and determinism as one of the defining characteristics of totalitarianism.

I should point out that Arendt describes totalitarian terror as a form of radical evil *not* in order to focus our attention simply on its scale or even on its methods. Writing in 1951 she reminds us that "many things that nowadays have become the specialty of totalitarian government are only too well known from the study of history" (*OT*, 440). Wars of aggression, massacres, even concentration camps (invented by the British during the Boer War) are all instrumentalities of terror familiar from the study of history. What Arendt wants us to appreciate is that terror is no mere *means* deployed by totalitarian governments; rather, it constitutes *their very essence* (*OT*, 464). This, of course, raises the question of whether the totalitarian form of government even *has* an essence, let alone a distinctive one. Arendt emphatically thinks that it does, and it is this claim more than any other that distinguishes her work.

In what sense, then, is terror the essence, rather than simply an instrument, of totalitarian government? Answering this question demands that we focus our attention on the fundamental but oft-overlooked theoretical difference that separates *tyrannical* from authentically *totalitarian* regimes. In the concluding chapter of *OT* Arendt notes that totalitarian government has effectively "exploded" the "very alternative on which all definitions of the essence of government have been based in political philosophy," namely, that between *lawful* and *lawless* government (or between "arbitrary" and "legitimate" power):

> It is the monstrous, yet seemingly unanswerable claim of totalitarian rule that, far from being "lawless," it goes to the sources of authority from which positive laws received their ultimate legitimation, that far from being arbitrary it is more obedient to these suprahuman forces than any government ever was before, and that far from wielding its power in the interest of one man, it is quite prepared to sacrifice everybody's vital immediate interests to the execution of what it assumes to be the law of History or the law of Nature. (*OT*, 461–2)

It is important to recognize that, unlike the "higher" laws typically appealed to by the Western tradition (Divine Law, Natural Law, time-honored custom, etc.) the laws of History or Nature obeyed by the totalitarians are first and foremost *laws of movement*. The fundamental "truth" underlying them is reality conceived as an all-consuming process, one whose motion and direction is determined by these laws. While Nature or History are ostensibly goal-directed processes that ultimately produce an "end product"—a transformed human species—considered as evolutionary processes they are, in fact, *endless*. There is and can be no end to the motion of either.

Totalitarian politics therefore assumes the characteristic form of a radical *movement* bent on undermining, co-opting, or neutralizing all stable legal-institutional forms in the home country. Once in power, totalitarian regimes extend this general policy to annexed or conquered lands. Now, however, the goal is not to simply co-opt or neutralize, but to *destroy* all relatively permanent laws and institutions. The removal of such "artificial" impediments clears the way for acceleration of the "laws of movement," first on a continental basis, and later—ideally—on a global one.

If we view their destructiveness in light of their ideological aspirations, it becomes clear that totalitarian regimes represent less the triumph of an unfettered politics than the ascendancy of a radical form of *anti-politics*. This anti-politics is manifest in their suspension or undermining of positive law and rights, their destruction of political and personal freedom, and their elimination of the idea that the status of being human endows one with anything like intrinsic worth. As Arendt notes, it is "for the sake of complete consistency" that "it is necessary for totalitarianism to destroy every trace of what we commonly call human dignity" (*OT*, 458).

Only when human beings are reduced to a plastic and malleable mass, prepared by terror and propaganda to take on the role of either executioner or victim, does it become possible to bring reality into complete accord with the dictates of the ideology. And, while the ideological "supersense" of a "naturally just" Aryan racial supremacy or a "historically just" classless utopia may be "ridiculous," the fact remains that the Nazis *succeeded* in reorganizing continental Europe in accordance with their racial principles, just as the Bolsheviks *succeeded* in eliminating the old social classes and collectivizing the Soviet Union. These regimes didn't just talk about "alternative facts." They *created* them, from the ground up, first and foremost by attempting to change human nature in order to "fabricate" a new animal species, mankind. That is why their essence was, and had to be, terror.

The European roots of totalitarianism

Arendt thinks that it is only by focusing our attention on the sheer radicality and novelty of totalitarian aims and methods that we can begin the work of comprehending what otherwise appears incomprehensible. But while there is a veritable chasm between totalitarian regimes and more familiar forms of domination, these regimes did not fall from the heavens nor emerge, fully formed, from hell. They were creatures born of European history and culture. What made their actualization possible was their appropriation and exploitation of ideas, attitudes, and practices that circulated widely in pre- and inter-war Europe. The pathologies that gave rise to these regimes—imperialism, racism, and anti-Semitism—were *European* pathologies. To look for their roots in the waywardness of a particular national culture or history is to miss the forest for the trees.

What, then, are the "elements" that formed the constellation in which totalitarianism (or something like it) became possible? In a 1946 outline she drew up for her publisher Arendt listed five: "antisemitism, decay of the national state, racism, expansion for expansion's sake, alliance between mob and capital" (MC, 28). "Expansion for expansion's sake" refers to European imperialism in the period between 1880 and 1914, a project that utilized race and racism as recurrent legitimations for unlimited conquest. The "decay of the nation-state" refers to the loss of territorial and political integrity experienced by European nation-states caught up in the imperialist project, while "the alliance between mob and capital" refers to the symbiosis that occurred when "superfluous capital" enlisted "superfluous labor" (lumpenproletariat elements from Europe) to serve as shock troops in the early stages of imperialist land grabs and subsequent pillaging of resources in Africa and elsewhere.

Arendt presents European imperialism as the outgrowth of what she refers to as "the political emancipation of the bourgeoisie." Contrary to Marx's claim that bourgeois interests determined governmental policy throughout the 19th century, Arendt argues that the bourgeoisie was notably uninterested in political or public affairs in the first half of the century (they were too busy making money). However, by the latter half of the 19th century, investment opportunities in the Western world had precipitously declined and "surplus money" in the form of excess or "superfluous" capital was forced to look elsewhere. The business imperatives of continuous economic growth and accumulation of profit drove a demand for new markets, raw materials, and cheaper sources of labor. "Imperialism," Arendt writes, "was born when the ruling class in capitalist production (the bourgeoisie) came up against national limitations to its economic expansion . . ." (*OT*, 126).

One result of these limitations was that *territorial expansion* came to be seen as critical to *business expansion*. The once apolitical bourgeoisie suddenly became interested in the conduct of the nation-state's foreign policy. Previously determined by balance of power considerations, the foreign policy of the major European nation-states came increasingly to be shaped by the apparent imperative of accumulating as much new territory (and as much surplus power) as possible. The age of imperialism—which reached its apogee with the so-called "scramble for Africa" in the late 1880s—commenced. The European nation-state, a political form hitherto characterized by the attachment of a particular ethnic people to a particular place in the world, now oriented itself toward "expansion for expansion's sake."

Sketched in such broad outline, it may seem that Arendt's story isn't all that different from Marx's. Each theorist sees the so-called "universality" of the state as given the lie by the concrete hegemony exercised by society's dominant class, the bourgeoisie. Arendt's version of the story seems merely to have delayed the historical moment when the state becomes the "ruling committee of the bourgeoisie" by a few decades.

Though understandable, such a response neglects a crucial feature of Arendt's account. While the "political emancipation of the bourgeoisie" is the catalyst of European expansionism, Arendt thinks that full-fledged imperialism emerges only when economic concepts migrate to the *political sphere*. There they begin to take on a life, and logic, of their own. The European nation-state system, predicated on the need to maintain a balance of power, gives way to a vision of the political world in which states appear as "fully-armed business concerns" engaged in an endless struggle for ever more territory and power. "Expansion as a permanent and supreme aim of politics," Arendt writes, "is the central idea of imperialism" (*OT*, 125).

By the latter half of the 19th century, a substantial portion of the wealth of European nation-states had been funneled into overseas investments. Where so much was at risk, it soon became clear to investors and statesmen alike that reliance upon the kind of security provided by lumpenproletariat adventurers (the "mob") was no longer tenable. The nation-state's army and police forces were obliged to step in.

What became of the "mob elements" once their role had been usurped by the armed forces of the nation-state? Some returned home. Many more—together with thousands of other "superfluous men" from Europe—were drawn to South Africa, first by the discovery of diamond fields (1867) and then gold (1884). There they became acquainted with the race society that had been established by the Boers, the all but forgotten descendants of 18th-century Dutch colonists. For Arendt, the Boers represent European man's discovery of *race* as a substitute for the *nation,* a discovery later 19th-century fortune seekers would carry with them back to Europe, with calamitous results.

Of course, the supposed political significance of race had been "discovered" by various European writers, starting with the Comte de Boulainvilliers in the 18th century and Arthur de Gobineau in the 19th. For these writers, race was first and foremost a *concept* that explained a given state of affairs. For Boulainvilliers, it explained the declining power of a "Frankish" aristocracy vis-à-vis a French majority descended from Latinized Gauls; for Gobineau, it explained the natural "superiority" of white Europeans relative to "inferior" Asians and Africans while simultaneously revealing the existential threat the latter posed to the "master race" through miscegenation.

However, as Arendt reminds us, "there is an abyss between men of brilliant and facile conceptions and men of brutal deeds and active bestiality which no intellectual explanation is able to bridge" (*OT*, 184). The bridging of this abyss depended upon experiences and the emergence of a political constellation that men like Gobineau could hardly have imagined, let alone foreseen.

The fundamental *experience* was the shock felt by Europeans when, like the Boers before them, they encountered a "wild" continent evidently teeming with "savages." A way of grasping and organizing this seeming chaos had to be found. The Boers provided the precedent. They were the first Europeans in Africa to employ race as an "emergency explanation of human beings who no European . . . could understand and whose humanity so frightened the [Dutch] immigrants that they no longer cared to belong to the same human species." Race was their answer to the "overwhelming monstrosity of Africa," and it was race that served as the basis of the brutally hierarchical society they created through enslavement of the native peoples. These peoples appeared to later European imperialists as they did to the Boers: as members of the same animal species, perhaps, but as merely *natural* men whose apparent lack of civilization made them something less than fully human.

The *political constellation* that helped bridge the gap between racist theory and racist practice was born of the imperialists' need for some mechanism capable of governing the large native populations in their more "civilized" colonial possessions (such as India). Both problems—the problem of how to understand and organize the "monstrosity" of Africa, and the problem of how to govern large native populations—were solved, Arendt thinks, by the discovery of what she calls "two new devices for political organization and rule over foreign peoples" during the 1880s:

> One was *race* as a principle of the body politic and the other *bureaucracy* as a principle of foreign domination. Without race as a substitute for the *nation*, the scramble for Africa and investment fever might well have remained the purposeless "dance of death and trade" [Conrad] of all gold rushes. Without bureaucracy as a substitute for *government* the British possession of India might well have been left to the recklessness of the "breakers of law" [Burke] without changing the political climate of an entire era. (*OT*, 185)

It was the race society created by the Boers that allowed more recently arrived Europeans to see "with their own eyes how peoples could be converted into races and how, simply by taking the initiative in this process, one might push one's own people into the position of the master race"—something they themselves would do, first in their new African possessions and later in Europe itself (*OT*, 206). And it was the "bureaucratic rule by decree" invented by men like Lord Cromer, the British Consul-General in Egypt from 1883 to 1907, that provided an effective "substitute for government" over populations that the imperial powers had no intention of recognizing as members of the nation-state or worthy of representation. The melding of these two devices created the racialized form of bureaucratic rule so characteristic of the British and French colonial empires, an imperialist invention later adopted by the totalitarians for use in Europe.

This brings us to one of the more arresting and influential ideas in *OT*. Arendt contends that the "overseas imperialism" of the western European powers spawned racist attitudes and governing practices that boomeranged back to Europe itself, undermining the idea of equal citizenship under the law that we associate with all post-French Revolution constitutional states (whether these be republican or monarchical in form). Increasingly, race and ethnicity came to define political membership, just as bureaucratic decree and police power came to substitute for lawful government.

The situation was exacerbated by the fact that, during the same period, politicians and ordinary people in central and eastern Europe came to share the overseas imperialists' generalized contempt for the narrow limits of the nation-state. They felt that they too had a "God-given right" to expansion. However, unlike their western counterparts, *their* dreams of expansion were focused not on overseas acquisitions but rather on the European land mass itself. The territorial ambitions of these "continental imperialists" were driven not only by the desire for increased natural resources and *Lebensraum* but also by what Arendt calls the "enlarged tribal consciousness" of ethnic groups in central, southern, and eastern Europe. These groups were nationalistic in orientation but, as subjects of multinational empires, they lacked a nation-state and political history of their own. Such inchoate nationalism received its classic articulation in the ideologies of Pan-Germanism and Pan-Slavism.

Pan-German and Pan-Slav sentiment grew in the wake of the revolutions of 1848. However, it crystallized into political movements only in the 1880s (*OT*, 222). Both movements were based on the idea that people of "similar folk origin"—that is, those who shared a similar language and culture—should be united, regardless of history and whatever political boundaries actually separated them. Thus, all German speakers—whether in Austria, Germany, Switzerland, or Czechoslovakia—should come together to form a "Greater Germany." Similarly, all people who spoke a Slavic language (and who possessed a Slavic "soul") should fight for independence from their German, Austro-Hungarian, or Ottoman overlords in order to unite with their "brother Slavs."

Arendt sees the pan-movements and continental imperialism as crucial elements in the constellation that made totalitarianism possible for three main reasons. First, because she believes that "Nazism and Bolshevism owe more to Pan-Germanism and Pan-Slavism (respectively) than to any other ideology or political movement" (*OT*, 222). Second, because they served as a vehicle for popular expansionist energies and a growing desire to efface the "artificial" political boundaries imposed by multinational empires. Third, and perhaps most importantly, because these movements were responsible for transforming the way millions of people in southern, central, and eastern Europe thought about political membership and identity.

Unlike their peers in western Europe, the ethnic minorities comprising the belt of mixed populations stretching from the Baltic to the Balkans "had no country, no state, no historic achievements to show." They lacked the all-important trinity of people–territory–state that, historically speaking, grounded the development of their western counterparts. If these minorities wanted to experience a national pride akin to their western European peers, they could "only point to themselves, and that meant, at best, to their language . . . at worst, to their Slavic or German, or God-knows-what soul" (*OT*, 232). This meant that their national and political identity became, almost by default, "more a portable private matter, inherent in their very personality, rather than a matter of public concern and civilization" (*OT*, 231). Political identity—which in the constitutional nation-states of western Europe received worldly articulation in terms of law, public institutions, and a shared political history—became something inner, pre-rational, and (as it were) "natural."

This is the background of the specifically *tribal* form of nationalism cultivated by the pan-movements. As if to compensate for the lack of both territory and state, these movements synthesized imperialist claims to national superiority with racist claims (such as the Boers') to a singular natural or divine origin. Regardless of whether one thought of one's people as chosen by God or Nature, the result was the same: peoples were transformed into animal species, "so that a Russian appears as different from a German as a wolf from a fox" (*OT*, 234). This splitting up of mankind into different ethnic-racial "species" not only ran contrary to the Judeo-Christian tradition's understanding of the divine origin of Man. It also effectively demolished the Enlightenment idea of humanity and the allied notion of a shared responsibility for the world.

When we combine this pseudo-naturalization of political identity with an inveterate hostility to *state institutions* and the *parliamentary system*, we are in better position to appreciate the full extent of the pan-movements' contribution to the political-cultural constellation that made totalitarianism possible. The pan-movements' hostility to state institutions flowed from the fact that these institutions, responsible for enforcing equal justice under the law, were identified with hated imperial overlords. Their hostility toward the parliamentary system flowed from the fact that parliamentary parties were representative of specific class interests, whereas the pan-movements claimed to speak for "the people" themselves. Prefiguring later totalitarian political movements, the pan-movements positioned themselves not only "above the parties" but also "above the state." Parliamentary politics and state institutions were viewed as illegitimate by movements that saw themselves as above sectional interests and above legal structures that failed to express German "blood" or the Slavic "soul."

The appearance of the pan-movements in central, eastern, and southern Europe was a function of the fact that, in the Austro-Hungarian and Russian empires, state structures had developed independently of a "nation" or ethnic majority people. These empires were truly multinational in character, and it is hardly fortuitous that the growth of nationalist sentiment in these parts of Europe fed an increasingly intense hatred of "alien" state structures and institutions. But what about the nation-states of western Europe, those countries fortunate enough to possess the "trinity" of people–territory–state rather than an agglomeration of "rootless" peoples *without* either a territory or state of their own? Shouldn't these have been pillars of stability in the otherwise chaotic years following the World War I?

To some degree constitutional nation-states like France did provide stability to a rapidly changing European order. However, the model they provided—that of a nation-state grounded in the tie between a specific ethnic majority and a particular place in the world—proved disastrous when the peace treaties concluding World War I extended the principle of self-determination to the "belt of mixed populations" between the Baltic and the Balkans. In these lands, the ethnic populations were too mixed up territorially to allow for the successful establishment of stable nation-states.

Thus, in newly formed political entities like Czechoslovakia, a national majority people (the Czechs) were allied to a "partner people" (the Slovaks) who were de facto second-class citizens. Moreover, special legal protections had to be created for the safeguarding of ethnic minorities (e.g. German speakers and Jews) from the newly empowered majority peoples. The ultimate effect of applying the principle of popular self-determination—the grounding principle of the nation-state—to these regions was to proliferate *classes* of citizenship as well as *legal statuses* for ethnic minorities who were deemed to require special protections within the newly constituted nation-states.

From Arendt's point of view, the replacement of an inclusive or "universal" form of political membership by classes of citizenship and special statuses was bad enough. With the refugee crisis following World War I—millions had been expelled from their home countries as the result of war, revolution, and civil war—the proliferation of *degrees* of political-civil membership (full citizens, "partner" people, protected minorities, resident aliens, stateless people or *apatrides*) intensified, and not only in such newly formed political entities as Czechoslovakia or a "restored" Poland.

Millions of displaced and denationalized people (Russians, Jews, Spaniards, southern and eastern Slavs) had no alternative but to seek refuge in the established nation-states of central and western Europe. The presence of increasing numbers of stateless refugees in nation-states like France—the historical home of equality under law, republican citizenship, and the "universal" Rights of Man—revealed a fundamental tension at the heart of the nation-state (Figure 5). This is the tension between the *state* (considered as "supreme legal institution" and guarantor of rights and civil equality) and the *nation* (the specific "self-determining" ethnic people that is both sovereign and the ultimate source of positive law). Arendt devotes some of her most arresting pages to the delineation of this "contradiction," a contradiction whose roots lie in what she calls the "perplexities" of the Rights of Man.

"The Declaration of the Rights of Man at the end of the eighteenth century," Arendt writes, "was a turning point in history":

> Since the Rights of Man were proclaimed to be "inalienable," irreducible to and undeducible from other rights or laws, no

5. Wartime refugees, Gare de Lyon, Paris, 1914.

> authority was invoked for their establishment: Man himself was their source as well as their ultimate goal. No special law, moreover, was deemed necessary to protect them because all laws were supposed to rest upon them. Man appeared as the only sovereign in matters of law as the people was proclaimed the only sovereign in matters of government. The people's sovereignty . . . was not proclaimed by the grace of God but in the name of Man, so that it seemed only natural that the "inalienable" rights of Man would find their guarantee and become an inalienable part of the right of the people to sovereign self-government. (*OT*, 291)

But this enormous stride forward in what Kant famously described as "man's emergence from his self-incurred tutelage" came at a price. No sooner had man "appeared as a completely emancipated, completely isolated being who carried his dignity within himself" than he "disappeared once again into a member of the people." What Arendt calls "the whole question of human rights" became inextricably linked to the question of national emancipation. Only the "emancipated sovereignty of the people, of one's own people, seemed able to insure" such rights (*OT*, 291).

In this way, *human* rights quickly came to be identified with the rights of *national peoples* within the European nation-state system. In practice, the "inalienable rights" all men supposedly carried within themselves turned out to be fictions the moment they were detached from the rights of a specific national (sovereign) *people*.

The baneful implications of this identification of the rights of man with the rights of national peoples were fully exposed by the interwar refugee crisis. Masses of people suddenly appeared "whose elementary rights were as little safeguarded in the ordinary functioning of nation-states in the middle of Europe as they would have been in the heart of Africa" (*OT*, 291). The comity of European nations broke down with the emergence of revolutionary and fascist regimes whose conception of sovereignty legitimated the summary denationalization of entire populations who had long lived within their borders. The stateless person, once a kind of "legal freak," became a ubiquitous presence, one whose elementary rights no sovereign nation-state was willing to guarantee.

It's at this point in her analysis that Arendt introduces her celebrated notion of the "right to have rights":

> We become aware of the existence of a right to have rights (and that means to live in a framework where one is judged by one's actions and opinions) and a right to belong to some kind of organized community, only when millions of people emerged who had lost and could not regain these rights because of the new global political situation. The trouble is that this calamity arose not from any lack of civilization, backwardness, or mere tyranny, but, on the contrary, that it could not be repaired because there was no longer any "uncivilized" spot on earth, because whether we like it or not we have really started to live in One World. Only with a completely organized humanity could the loss of home and political status become identical with expulsion from humanity altogether. (*OT*, 296–7)

Those who had been denationalized *en masse* or forced to emigrate by civil war and revolution have no place to go in the world which was *not* a sovereign nation-state; nowhere, that is, that did not enforce the practical principle that *only nationals can have rights* (regardless of whatever "theoretical" commitment to human rights or the "Rights of Man" may be found in their constitutions or political rhetoric). "The conception of human rights," Arendt writes, "based on the assumed existence of a human being as such, broke down the moment when those who professed to believe in it were for the first time confronted with people who had indeed lost all other qualities and specific relationships, except that they were still human." The sad fact of the matter was that "the world found nothing sacred in the abstract nakedness of being human" (*OT*, 299–300).

Arendt's analysis goes a long way to explaining how it was that millions of stateless people between the wars came to be viewed as "useless mouths" or superfluous people. In light of this analysis, we might well expect Arendt to urge us to recognize a universal and inclusive "right to have rights" and to recommit, theoretically and practically, to the idea of human rights that emerged with (but was imperfectly formulated by) the 1789 "Declaration of the Rights of Man and the Citizen." And that, indeed, is the preponderant moral force of her argument. However, it comes with a crucial qualification. This is Arendt's notable *skepticism* toward the very idea of so-called "natural rights," rights individual human beings have been endowed with by either Nature or God:

> When the Rights of Man were proclaimed for the first time, they were regarded as being independent of history and the privileges which history had accorded certain strata of society.... Historical rights were replaced by natural rights, "nature" took the place of history, and it was tacitly assumed that nature was less alien than history to the essence of man... Today we are perhaps better qualified to judge exactly what this human "nature" amounts to... Ever since a deeper knowledge of natural processes instilled serious

> doubts about the existence of natural laws at all, nature has assumed a sinister aspect. How should one be able to deduce laws and rights from a universe which apparently knows neither one or the other? (*OT*, 298)

Dogmatic assertions about "inalienable rights" and "the dignity of man" ring hollow in light of a nature that has been stripped of all normative significance. Nor is the appeal to history and what Hegel called "progress in the consciousness of freedom" much help. Arendt thinks that "history and nature have become equally alien to us, namely in the sense that the essence of man can no longer be comprehended in terms of either category" (*OT*, 298).

Does Arendt propose a new ground for determining "the essence of man" and (thus) for the reality of universal human rights? The answer here is emphatically no. Arendt's position is that *equality* is not something natural or "God-given." Rather, equality is "the result of human organization insofar as it is guided by the principle of justice." It is, in a word, *artificial*, a function of legal persona and membership in political associations committed to the principle of equal treatment under the law. "We are not born equal," Arendt writes, "we become equal on the strength of our decision to guarantee ourselves mutually equal rights" (*OT*, 301). That is why she characterizes the "right to have rights" in terms not just of a right to *membership* of some "organized community," but as a right to "live in a framework where one is judged by one's actions and opinions" rather than by one's group identity.

Where, then, does one turn if "neither natural law, nor divine command, nor any [normative] concept of mankind" can convincingly ground the idea of a "right to have rights"? The only answer, Arendt suggests in *OT*, is humanity itself—humanity not as a "regulative idea" but as an "inescapable fact" born of the reality of an interconnected, and fully inhabited, world. In this situation humanity has "in effect assumed the role formerly ascribed to nature or history."

This means that the "right to have rights," if it is to be guaranteed at all, must be "guaranteed by humanity itself"—by a humanity that has "come of age" by virtue of having become a concrete (globalized) reality. As Arendt notes, "it is by no means certain whether this is possible," especially given the underdeveloped state of international law and the relative scarcity of federative structures between states (*OT*, 298–300).

From totalitarian movements to totalitarianism in power

Arendt's analyses of the ways in which imperialism, racism, bureaucratic rule by decree, and the "perversion" of the state into a tool of the nation all expand our understanding of how certain attitudes, practices, and events helped shape a European context in which totalitarianism became possible. But the second part of *OT* leaves some key questions unanswered. First, how is it that totalitarian movements came to enjoy the mass support that helped propel them to power? Second, what makes totalitarian ideology, propaganda, and organization at once so distinctive and effective? And third, what role did anti-Semitism play in amalgamating the various "elements" that crystallized into totalitarianism? The first two questions are answered in Part Three of *OT*, while the third refers us back to Part One ("Anti-Semitism").

Arendt answers the first question by examining the historical-sociological situation confronted by a large number of ordinary Europeans in the interwar period (1918–38). Her thesis is that the catastrophe of World War I—which led to the collapse of the German *Kaiserreich* as well as the Austro-Hungarian and Russian empires—combined with the economic collapse born of the Great Depression to destroy the web of relationships and interests that had constituted the European class system. The relatively secure class positions of millions dissolved almost overnight. Newly "rootless" *masses* now took the place of politically organized and socially integrated *peoples*.

It was from these masses that totalitarian movements drew their strength. Those who joined them typically did not come from the ranks of the parliamentary parties, nor did they emerge from the European working class. Between the elites of the old party system and the organized working class lay a large group of lower-middle-class property owners and shopkeepers who had been ruined—first by a series of investment scandals in the 1880s and 1890s, then again (and more devastatingly) by the Great Depression in the 1930s. Such people, clearly distinct from *déclassé* "mob" elements, had constituted a "slumbering majority" during the preceding half-century of class-based parliamentary politics in Europe. Uninterested in public affairs, this majority awakened politically only when it became clear that the established order was utterly incapable of protecting either their social position or livelihoods.

Bereft of the "normal social relationships" that their place in class society once afforded them, the lonely and atomized individuals who comprised the "modern masses" were attracted to radically anti-bourgeois, anti-parliamentary political parties. As Arendt observes, "totalitarian movements are possible wherever there are masses who for one reason or another have acquired the taste for political organization" (*OT*, 311). It was this previously apathetic and politically unorganized mass that provided the Nazi and Communist movements with their most reliable supporters.

Arendt's recurring characterizations of "the masses" as rootless, alienated, and atomized brings Tocqueville to mind. But while there are certainly echoes of Tocqueville in Arendt's analysis there are also clear differences. First, the atomization of the "mass man" Arendt describes in *OT* is not produced by the rise of democratic equality; rather, it is the result of the dissolution of a class society which had remained intact long after equality before the law had established itself in constitutional republics and monarchies. This dissolution was brought about by successive shocks—war, revolution, economic collapse, civil war—which, as noted above, left many in the middle and lower-middle classes lacking not only resources but a secure place in the social world.

Secondly, the reaction of people in these groups to economic shocks and loss of social standing was *not* a retreat to the little world of family, friends, and private affairs. It was, rather, a seething anger at institutions, elites, and political leaders who had either failed in the breach or who were deemed responsible for the serial political and economic catastrophes in the first place.

It's at this point of maximum alienation from parliamentary politics that the "slumbering majorities" of shopkeepers, tradesmen, and small business owners begin to "acquire a taste for political organization." Given the circumstances, it is perhaps not surprising that many were attracted to violently anti-bourgeois, anti-liberal political movements. What is surprising is how *selflessness*, hitherto a relatively rare human quality, now became a mass phenomenon. Once the millions reduced to straitened material circumstances were added to the vast numbers who had perished in World War I, the "rational pursuit of self-interest"—a fundamental presupposition of bourgeois society and its parliamentary system—seemed to lose all meaning. A world beset by cascading political and economic disasters turned the very idea of such pursuit into a cruel joke.

Among the masses this situation produced what Arendt describes as a "radical loss of self-interest" and a "cynical or bored indifference in the face of death or other personal catastrophes." This indifference to their own fate combined with a "passionate inclination toward the most abstract notions as guides for life" and a "general contempt for even the most obvious rules of common sense" (*OT*, 316). Psychologically speaking, what was needed was some idea or narrative that could explain the traumas of the present, the significance of the past, and the direction or *telos* of the future. This is what the ideological fictions of Nazism and Bolshevism provided: a single idea—that of race or class struggle—that could serve as the key to the past while confidently predicting, with pseudo-scientific accuracy, the shape of the future.

The totalitarians believed that there were hidden forces at work in history—"secret conspiracies" hatched by international capitalism, Trotskyites, or Jews—and their propaganda relentlessly trumpeted the responsibility these conspiracies bore for creating the hardships faced by ordinary people. Never mind the fact that such conspiracies were complete fictions. What mattered was their ability to "explain" a reality whose unpredictable swings made life all but unbearable for the average individual. The rigorous consistency with which the totalitarians "deduced" the meaning of past and present events from a single premise (race or class struggle) made their ideologies singularly attractive to masses who found it virtually impossible to make sense of the chaos of their own lived experience.

Arendt cites the ability of totalitarian movements to "shut the masses off from the real world" by means of ideology and propaganda lies as one reason for their astonishing success:

> Before they seize power and establish a world according to their doctrines, totalitarian movements conjure up a lying world of total consistency which is more adequate to the needs of the human mind than reality itself; in which, through sheer imagination, uprooted masses can feel at home and are spared the never-ending shocks which real life and real experiences deal to human beings and their expectations. (*OT*, 353)

The masses' "longing for fiction" is fulfilled by such a "lying world of total consistency." However, it is important to note two things about Arendt's analysis. First, it is not the case that *any* fiction will fulfill this need. The "enemies of the people" targeted by totalitarian propaganda must be grounded in some historical-empirical reality. Jewish financiers, like international capitalists and Trotskyites, did exist, even if their conspiracy for world domination was a complete fiction. Second, it is not as if the masses were child-like in their naïveté, innocent victims of fiendishly clever propagandists like Joseph Goebbels. Rather, their disillusionment produced a curious mix of cynicism and gullibility: "In an ever-changing, incomprehensible world, the masses had reached the point where they would, at the same time, believe everything and nothing, think that everything was possible and that nothing was true" (*OT*, 382).

The masses accepted the faithlessness and repeated volte-faces of their leaders as readily as they accepted conspiracy theories about Jews and Trotskyites. Gullible and cynical, they swallowed the speeches and lies the regime prepared for public consumption. When the leader abruptly reversed course, they pretended they knew all along it was just a clever ruse (the Hitler–Stalin pact of 1939 is a good example). Belief in the leader's omniscience and infallibility was undergirded by his ability to "predict" events (such as the destruction of European Jewry or the disappearance of a "dying" class) with pseudo-scientific accuracy, an accuracy later "confirmed" by the deadly measures taken to directly produce the "foreseen" result.

The cultivation of such belief, combined with the masses' longing for fiction, enabled totalitarian movements to demand and receive something "all other parties and movements" never even dreamed of: total loyalty. According to Arendt, total loyalty is the "psychological basis" of "total domination"—a form of domination possible only where there are large numbers of "atomized, isolated, individuals." "Such loyalty," she observes, "can be expected only from the completely isolated human being who, without any other social ties to family, friends, comrades or even mere acquaintances derives his sense of having a place in the world only from his belonging to a movement, his membership in the party" (*OT*, 323). The distance between rulers and ruled is elided by a form of domination which does not rely on coercion alone but which dominates from *within*.

This brings us to the question of how totalitarianism is organized, first as a movement seeking power and then as a "so-called state." Arendt suggests that the most appropriate image for authentically authoritarian rule is a pyramid, a niched hierarchy with authority and power filtering down through the ranks from top to bottom. In contrast, the proper image of totalitarian rule and organization is an onion-like structure. In the center of the onion we find a kind of empty space where the leader is located:

> Whatever he does . . . he does from within, and not from without or above. All the extraordinarily manifold parts of the movement—the front organizations, the various professional societies, the party membership, the party bureaucracy, the elite formations, and the police groups—are related in such a way that each forms the facade in one direction and the center in the other, that is, plays the role of normal outside world for one layer and the role of radical extremism for another. The great advantage of this system is that the movement provides for each of its layers, even under the conditions of totalitarian rule, the fiction of a normal world along with the consciousness of being different from and more radical than it. (*BPF*, 99)

Thus, while totalitarian propaganda separates the masses from the "real world" by supplying ideological fiction, this separation is, in fact, relative. The further one penetrates the layers of the onion, the more radical the worldview and the greater the readiness for murderous action. The masses in Germany, for example, willingly accepted the fiction of a Jewish conspiracy along with the more abstract idea that all history was the history of race struggle. None of them, however, would have guessed that these two "facts" entailed either undertaking the physical extermination of European Jewry or starting a global struggle for world domination. The reason for the masses' "gullibility" on this count is simple: they accepted the public face of the Nazi movement, mistaking it as a conservative movement aiming at an authoritarian nationalism.

To the onion-like structure of the movement corresponds the planned shapelessness of the "so-called totalitarian state." Arendt deploys this characterization because she wants to draw our attention to the fact that there is no clear bureaucratic hierarchy or chain of command in totalitarian states. "One should never forget," she writes, "that only a building can have a structure, but that a movement can only have a direction" (*OT*, 398). The point of a movement is to *keep moving* with ever-greater momentum toward the goal posited by its ideological fiction. Stable state institutions with clear chains of authority can only impede this momentum. That is why, within the "so-called totalitarian state," ministries and offices were duplicated and reduplicated, to the point where it was never clear where actual power of decision actually lay.

Arendt wants us to see that it is not the state apparatus that wields power, but the party, whose increasingly radical directives come from the leader. The state as a "supreme legal institution"—the stability of which would have made something like normal life possible—effectively ceases to exist. It is destroyed from the inside through a profusion of overlapping ministries and bureaus, reduced to being little more than a facade presented to the outside world. Within the apparatus itself, the only *real* power resides with the secret police (the Gestapo or NKVD). These, of course, followed only orders originating from the highest ranks of the party or from the leader himself. The ubiquity of the secret police keeps the servants of the state apparatus off-balance and sycophantically loyal, fearful not just for their careers but their lives.

What role did anti-Semitism play in all this? The answer in the case of the Nazi movement seems obvious: the idea of a Jewish conspiracy for world domination was the centerpiece of their ideological fiction. However, the relevance of anti-Semitism to Soviet totalitarianism seems less clear. Did the horror of the Holocaust and the "industrial production of corpses" lead Arendt to exaggerate the importance of anti-Semitism in helping to bring about both forms of totalitarian rule?

A case could be made that she did. Here one must remember that she presents anti-Semitism as one *element* in the constellation of events, attitudes, and practices that contributed to making totalitarianism possible. Like racism and imperialism, it helped set the stage for the emergence of total domination as a regime form. However, Arendt thought that anti-Semitism played a unique role. It was, in her view, a *catalytic agent* crucial to the crystallization of the other elements in the constellation she describes.

Anti-Semitism could play this critical role because, like racism and imperialism, it was a pan-European phenomenon between 1880 and 1933 (the year of the Nazi seizure of power). During the last two decades of the 19th century anti-Semitism emerged as a *political ideology* (as distinct from social prejudice or religious hatred) for the first time. Again and again, we find anti-Semitism demonstrating its value as both mobilizing force and organizational tool. From the France of the Dreyfus Affair to the emergence of explicitly anti-Jewish political parties in Austria and Germany, to the masses' widespread belief in the authenticity of the "Protocols of the Elders of Zion," the appeal of anti-Semitism across classes and nationalities prior to World War I was undeniable. When it came to stirring up fears and focusing resentments, anti-Jewish propaganda proved itself extraordinarily potent.

Why the Jews, though? Arendt's attempt at an answer picks up on a hint offered by Tocqueville in *The Ancien Regime and the Revolution*. Why, Tocqueville asks, did the French people, in the period immediately preceding the Revolution, come to hate the aristocracy with an intensity never before seen? His answer is that this hatred was inversely proportional to the amount of power the aristocracy in fact wielded. The French aristocrat once filled important social, political, and legal roles at the local and regional level. He was the respected *seigneur* to the peasants, a powerful *parlementaire* to the bourgeoisie, and—as head of the manorial court—chief judge and upholder of the law in the towns and villages around his estate. However, when Louis XIV made Versailles the center of the social and political universe, the aristocracy abandoned its hitherto vital role in local and regional affairs, losing the bulk of the power it once wielded in the process. This rapid loss of power was not, however, accompanied by any real decline in their fortunes. Hatred of the aristocracy reached its zenith at this point, as the entire nation came to view the nobility as useless, overprivileged, and fundamentally parasitic.

Arendt suggests a similar dynamic was at work with respect to European Jewry. Like the French aristocracy, they too once played an important social and political role, one that tied them closely to the nation-state and its fate.

As a people, the Jews had long occupied a tenuous place in Europe. They were barred from numerous professions and subject to periodic outbursts of anti-Jewish violence. Nevertheless, established trading and financial networks stretching to the Middle East and orient enabled a significant number of Jews to prosper between these spasms of Christian violence. Yet their communities were and remained separate. Often relegated to ghettoes (such as those in Venice and Frankfurt) they were subject to laws and restrictions on their movements and activities that even the lowliest gentile was not.

The 17th and 18th centuries saw an important shift in the situation of European Jews. Under the tutelage of absolute monarchs, the fledging nation-states of western Europe underwent significant economic, military, and urban development. However, neither the aristocracy nor the nascent bourgeoisie were willing to partner with the state and provide the necessary capital loans for this development. Absolute monarchs turned increasingly to wealthy Jews as lenders of last resort, to the point where the "court Jew" became a familiar figure in European capitals. Wealthy Jews were accorded special privileges and exemptions by monarchs eager to protect what had become an indispensable financial arrangement.

When, after the French Revolution, nation-states in the modern sense emerged, the financial needs of their governments outstripped the resources such court Jews could supply. Only by pooling together the combined wealth of the better-off strata of western and central European Jewry could Jewish bankers begin to meet the state's demand for ever more credit and ever larger capital loans. This reliance upon the combined resources of the broader Jewish community ultimately resulted in the state granting emancipation to Jews in all but the most backward of countries.

The Jews were now "equal"—at least in the eyes of the state—but they remained excluded from the society at large. They themselves did not constitute a class (they "were neither workers, middle-class people, landholders, nor peasants"), nor would any class ally itself with them. Socially isolated, they remained dependent upon the state to protect their newly granted rights and to preserve certain long-standing privileges. As Arendt pointedly observes, "there is no doubt that the nation-state's interest in preserving the Jews as a special group and preventing their assimilation into class society coincided with the Jewish interest in self-preservation and group survival" (*OT*, 13).

The relationship between the Jews and the state changed profoundly with the dawn of the imperialist age. The bourgeoisie—who previously preferred private investments to the issuing of government credit—now became partners with national governments pursuing the imperialist project of "expansion for expansion's sake." The Jews' importance as a group correspondingly declined, even as some individual Jews maintained their positions as financial advisors and intra-European middlemen.

As the nation-state's institutional structure began to disintegrate with this territorial expansion, the state itself came under attack by resentful ethnic minorities and the increasingly disaggregated masses. Having staked the legitimacy of its position "above" class or sectional interests, the state's relationship vis-à-vis society became one of ever-increasing tension if not outright contradiction. As the hostility of the masses and ethnic minorities toward the state increased, so did hostility toward the Jews. The Jews were the one group that was neither part of the nation nor integrated into class society. Moreover, they were the one group that benefited (or seemed to benefit) from an especially intimate relationship with the increasingly hated state institutions.

Arendt's tying the fate of European Jews to that of the state as "supreme legal institution" is a penetrating insight, one that helps to explain how it was that anti-Semitism—a centuries-old social and religious phenomenon—suddenly became politicized at the end of the 19th century. The fact that anti-Semitism and anti-state feeling were two sides of the same coin, each shaping and defining the other, enabled the Pan-German and Pan-Slav movements to enlist the surge in anti-Semitic sentiment in their attack on the state's independence and all "artificial" legal-institutional boundaries. Like racism and imperialism, anti-Semitism had a trans-European appeal. Unlike racism and imperialism, however, anti-Semitic sentiment could be found spread across the political spectrum. Its value as a recruiting, organizing, and mobilizing tool was thus virtually unlimited. This fact scarcely went unnoticed by the totalitarian movements themselves.

Chapter 3
Political freedom, the public realm, and the *vita activa*

It should come as no surprise that, after expending so much effort analyzing the nature and roots of totalitarianism, Hannah Arendt should turn her attention to the topic of freedom. What *is* surprising is that this concern centers almost entirely upon public or political freedom, the freedom (in Thomas Jefferson's phrase) "to be a participator in the government of affairs." After *Origins*, Arendt became one of the foremost upholders of the dignity of politics, even going so far as to assert (in the words of one of her critics) the "existential supremacy of political action."

For most of us, the idea that someone who escaped totalitarian domination and the relentless politicization of everyday life should become a champion of what the Greeks called the *bios politikos*—the political way of life—cannot but appear strange. Arendt herself was aware of the apparent irony. She began her 1961 essay "What is Freedom?" by asking "was not the liberal credo, 'The less politics, the more freedom,' right after all?... Is it not true, as we all somehow believe, that politics is compatible with freedom only because and insofar as it guarantees a possible freedom *from* politics?" (*BPF*, 144–5). The latter type of freedom is the freedom from interference by political, social, and religious authorities who would treat us paternalistically and tell us how to live our lives.

Such "negative liberty" has long been at the core of the liberal tradition of political thought. From such proto-liberals as John Locke and Immanuel Kant, to such classic 19th-century figures as Benjamin Constant and J. S. Mill, to Arendt's contemporary Isaiah Berlin, the focus of writers in the liberal tradition has been on individual rights, liberties, and the value of *autonomy*—that is, on being able to pursue our "own good in our own way" (Mill) so long as we desist from harming the rights and vital interests of others.

Arendt's focus on public or political liberty flowed from her conviction that one key factor in the rise of totalitarianism was that so few Europeans had a sense of themselves as *citizens* engaged in the activity of self-government. Atomized by the decay of the European class system, resentful of political elites, and traumatized by war and economic collapse, they preferred ideological fiction and the destruction of the established *res publica* to its preservation and augmentation. Given this analysis, it is easy to see why Arendt thought a shared sense of responsibility for political institutions and the public world was the *sine qua non* of any healthy or humane political life. While the liberal tradition has had enormous historical success in promoting the ideas of limited government and individual rights, it has been notoriously deficient when it comes to cultivating an ethos of shared responsibility for, and active participation in, the public-political world.

This specific criticism of liberal thought links Arendt to civic republicanism, generally regarded as the second most influential tradition in the history of modern political thought. This tradition, whose roots can be traced back as far as Aristotle, contains a diverse set of figures—Machiavelli, James Harrington, Montesquieu, Rousseau, Jefferson, and Tocqueville (a "liberal" republican) among them. These thinkers diverge on numerous issues, but there is one point upon which they all agree: the fundamental importance of what Italian Renaissance humanists referred to as the *vivere civile*—the civil or political life. All these thinkers saw active civic participation as fundamental to the cultivation of a strong sense of the public good and a deeper appreciation of the value of political freedom. From the self-governing republics celebrated by Machiavelli and Guicciardini, to the strident anti-monarchical voices heard during the English Civil War, to (ultimately) the successful establishment of large-scale republics by the American and French Revolutions, the civic republican tradition has provided a robustly political counterpoint to the market- and rights-based individualism that underlies much of the liberal tradition.

In approaching Arendt's political theory for the first time, then, the reader should bear in mind her broad allegiance to the republican tradition, her many disagreements with some of its figures (e.g. Rousseau) notwithstanding. Doing so helps us avoid the misinterpretations of her thought that have plagued the reception of her work in Anglo-American circles. Chief among these is the image of Arendt as an unabashed Grecophile, an uncritical celebrant of the direct democracy of Periclean Athens who espouses a heroic-masculine conception of politics and political action.

The first step in avoiding such a misreading is to take Arendt at her word when she states (in the "Prologue" to *THC*) that her project in the book is to reconsider "the human condition from the vantage point of our newest experiences and our most recent fears" and to "think what we are doing" to *our* public sphere and the type of activities suited to appear in it (*THC*, 5). Placing this description front and center enables us to grasp the reasons for, and limits to, her turn to the Greeks as she attempts to distinguish *political* forms of speech and action from the more strategic and instrumental modes we are familiar with.

Rather than regard political action as simply a means to the increase of power or the advancement of interests, Arendt focuses on the inherent value of the activities of debate, deliberation, persuasion, and exchange of opinion. It is through such quintessentially political forms of speech that diverse citizens argue and decide matters of public or common concern. The activities of debate, deliberation, persuasion, and decision form the core of self-government, and "self-government under laws" is what republican government is all about.

Such self-government can be said to genuinely occur only when diverse citizens have equal access to public spaces for such debate, deliberation, and decision about common affairs. Arendt wants us to confront the fact that, by privileging activities connected to the economic "life process" of society over everything else, we have created a world in which such spaces have become vanishingly rare. The constitutional republic has been transformed into an economic polity, a form of association in which the activities of laboring and production take center stage, to the virtual exclusion of everything else.

THC's entry into consideration of these and other issues will no doubt strike many readers as oblique. In her "Prologue" Arendt begins by noting that the changes in the human condition made possible by modern science and technology have, for the most part, been little reflected upon in our political discourse. In part this is because ordinary speech is ill-equipped to deal with scientific complexities. But it is also because thoughtlessness has become, in Arendt's view, one of the "outstanding characteristics of our time" (5). When she proposes to "think what we are doing" the accent is plainly on the activities that comprise the "doing." Arendt calls "what we are doing" the "central theme" of her book, explaining that "it deals only with the most elementary articulations of the human condition, with those activities that traditionally, as well as according to current opinion, are within the range of every human being" (5).

These activities—labor, work, and action—are "general human capacities which grow out of the human condition and are permanent, that is, cannot be irretrievably lost so long as the human condition itself is not changed" (6). By highlighting the advent of the economic polity and continued revolutions in science and technology, Arendt is able to argue that the human condition is on the verge not just of change, but of far-reaching and perhaps decisive change. The very "general human capacities" we take for granted may be at risk. This is clearly the case with our capacity for initiatory or "spontaneous" action, but it might also be the case with our apparently less threatened capacities for labor and work. The evaporation of spaces for debate and deliberation, the replacement of durable artifacts ("the work of our hands") with rapidly devoured consumer goods, and the accelerating automation of the labor process signal profound changes to the three activities that have traditionally comprised the *vita activa*.

Before considering these changes and the threat they represent, however, we must first get a bit clearer about what Arendt means by "the human condition." The reader might assume that "the human condition" is an expression equivalent to "human nature." But that would be a mistake:

> The human condition is not the same as human nature, and the sum total of human activities and capabilities which correspond to the human condition does not constitute anything like human nature. For neither those we discuss here [labor, work, and action] nor those we leave out, like thought and reason... constitute essential characteristics of human existence in the sense that without them this existence would no longer be human. The most radical change in the human condition we can imagine would be an emigration of men from the earth to some other planet. Such an event, no longer totally impossible, would imply that man would have to live under man-made conditions, radically different from those the earth offers him. Neither labor nor work nor action nor, indeed, thought as we know it would then make sense any longer.

Yet even these hypothetical wanderers from the earth would still be human. (*THC*, 10)

With this caveat in mind, we are in a better position to understand Arendt's pairing of each "fundamental" human activity with a particular "human condition." The human condition of labor, she tells us, is "life itself," while the human condition of work is *worldliness*. Action, "the only activity that goes on directly between men without the intermediary of things or matter," is related to the human condition of *plurality*—to the fact that "men, and not Man, live on the earth and inhabit the world" (7).

In each case, Arendt is alerting us to a correspondence between one type of human activity and a specific "condition of human existence." Our capacity for labor "grows out of" the conditioning force of life itself (the need of the human body to reproduce both itself and its labor power on a daily basis), while our capacity for work grows out of the fact that we are *worldly* beings; that is, beings who exist not in a natural environment but rather within a "human artifice" produced by man in his role as fabricator (or *homo faber*). Our capacity for action—for spontaneous beginning, for unpredictable words and deeds determined neither by the needs of our bodies nor by strictly utilitarian considerations—grows out of and is made possible by the human condition of plurality.

Each of these human capacities is "permanent" in the sense that they cannot be lost "so long as the human condition itself is not changed." Yet Arendt thinks that we are witnessing such a change in the human condition. "Thinking what we are doing" is imperative not simply because we need to be reminded of distinctions between different *types* of human activities (distinctions which the modern age has consistently blurred). It is imperative because "what we are doing"—and have been doing for the past 300 years—is exercising our capacities for labor, work, and action in ways that significantly alter the conditions of our existence, putting some if not all of our most distinctively human characteristics at risk.

How does such an alteration in our existential conditions come about? According to Arendt, the process starts toward the end of the 17th/beginning of the 18th century with what she calls "the rise of the social." By this she means the increasingly public hegemony of economic activities and what she calls the "life process" of society itself. This hegemony has its roots in the rise of early modern capitalism and the demographic expansion that occurred during the mid-18th century.

Arendt draws our attention to the fact that viewing something called "society" as the self-evident referent of our economic, political, and cultural discourse is a relatively new phenomenon. It came about thanks to the early expansion of trade and the need to correspondingly scale up commodity production. It was this need that propelled productive activities such as weaving out of the household (the primary site of economic activity in earlier times) and into the factory. The dynamism of early modern capitalism—with its acceleration of production, increased demand for markets and raw materials, and relentless competition—dissolved the patriarchal ties between classes that had defined the hierarchy of the *ancien régime*. The resulting transformation dislodged the feudal model of an organic community held together by rank and privilege and replaced it with what appeared to be a collection of random individuals, each pressured by market forces to pursue their individual self-interest. However, as such early political economists as Adam Smith, David Ricardo, and James Mill never tired of pointing out, behind the atomization and apparent anarchy of the new order stood a complex system of trade and commodity production, a system integrated and directed by the "hidden hand" of the market. The resulting totality comprised the economic "life process" not just of disparate individuals, but of society itself.

Here we encounter what Arendt, following the Swedish economist Gunnar Myrdal, cites as the "communistic fiction" underlying classical political economy. The fiction is that of a unitary macro-subject, Society, whose life process not only constitutes the "material base" of the new order but also limns its horizon of value and experience. The truth of this observation can be seen from the fact that it is difficult if not impossible for us to talk about anything that isn't strictly personal without attaching the adjective "social" to it. We take it for granted that whenever we address political, economic, or cultural matters we are, in fact, talking about "society" or "social issues." The sheer pervasiveness of the category of "the social" thus makes it extraordinarily difficult to see the "rise of the social" as a *historical* phenomenon, one that fundamentally altered our perception of the public-political realm and the kinds of activities fit to appear within it.

It is this short-sightedness that Arendt aims to correct in *THC*'s second chapter, "The Public and the Private Realm." The point of this chapter is not to delineate essentialist conceptions of the public and private realms, and then to accuse the modern age and "the rise of the social" as illegitimately mixing the two. Admittedly, the text sometimes reads that way. Arendt begins by pointing out how Aristotle's famous definition of man as a "political animal" (*zōōn politikon*) was mistranslated by Thomas Aquinas as *animal socialis* (social animal)—a harbinger of the much later absorption of the political realm by the social. She then outlines the ancient Greek understanding of the political realm (or *polis*) as distinct from the household (or *oikos*). Her point in highlighting this distinction is not to argue that the Greeks got it right and that we should abandon our own view of the matter and return to theirs. Given the expansive nature of the modern economy and the brutally hierarchical nature of Greek household life, such a "return" is clearly neither plausible nor desirable.

One reason Arendt turns to the Greeks is that she wants to draw the sharpest possible contrast with *our* understanding of the public and private realms, a relationship we see framed in terms of the broader category of "the social." For the Greeks, the household—the place where all activities related to material or biological reproduction occurred—was a realm determined by the necessity imposed by life itself. It was therefore characterized by the strictest inequality. The male head of household stood as master over the subsistence-oriented economic activity performed by women, slaves, and children. It was only when the household head stepped *outside* this space of necessity-determined inequality and into the public realm that he encountered his equals: *other* male heads of households on their way to the agora or assembly, there to debate issues relating to the domestic or foreign policy of the *polis*.

The moment he crossed the boundary separating the private realm from the public, the household master was transformed into one citizen among many equals. The political activities he and his peers engaged in—the speech and action they performed as members of the assembly, in the agenda-setting executive council, or in the large juries known as *dikasteries*—were free activities, in no way determined by biological necessity or the coercive force wielded by a ruler or ruling class. It is commonplace to observe that the Greeks invented democracy. But it is also true to say that they invented *politics*—that is, the process of deliberating and deciding common matters publicly, through persuasive speech, rather than by coercive force or a monopoly on public power (the mode favored by the Greek *tyrannos* and the "Great King" who ruled the Persian Empire).

Characterizing the Greek understanding of the difference between the *oikos* and the *polis* as one between the "realm of necessity" and the "realm of freedom" allows Arendt to draw a sharp distinction between the types of activities appropriate to both. All laboring activities relating directly to the "life process"—to economic and biological reproduction—were, for the Greeks, relegated to the private realm, while all genuinely political activities occurred in the spaces that constituted the public realm (the assembly, the agora, etc.). It is of the utmost importance to Arendt that the Greeks understood freedom as something essentially public and political in nature. It was only later, with the decline of *polis* life and the growth of alienation from the world under the Roman imperium, that Stoic philosophers and early Christian writers transformed what had once been the visible *fact* of public-political freedom into the invisible (and strictly personal) *problem* of "freedom of the will."

Arendt's position on the "question" of human freedom and its original location is neatly summed up in "What is Freedom?":

> The field where freedom has always been known, not as a problem, to be sure, but as a fact of everyday life, is the political realm. And even today, whether we know it or not, the question of politics and the fact that man is a being endowed with the gift of action must always be present to our mind when we speak of the problem of freedom; for action and politics, among all the capabilities and potentialities of human life, are the only things we could not even conceive without at least assuming that freedom exists... Freedom, moreover, is not only one among the many problems and phenomena of the political realm properly speaking, such as justice, or power, or equality; freedom, which only seldom—in times of crisis or revolution—becomes the direct aim of political action, is actually the reason that men live together in political organization at all. Without it, political life would be meaningless. The *raison d'être* of politics is freedom, and its field of experience of action. (*BPF*, 144–5)

I quote this passage at length because it articulates one of Arendt's most fundamental convictions, namely, that tangible freedom is to be found where many of us least expect it: in the public-political realm. This of course assumes a public-political realm founded upon some version of civic equality, since relations of domination are not, in Arendt's view, *political* relations at all.

Arendt rehearses the Greek distinction between the (public) "realm of freedom" and the (private) "realm of necessity," the better to highlight her contrastive understanding of the nature of freedom. Human freedom can become a tangible reality only given the availability of a legally and institutionally bounded public realm. This artificial or "worldly" edifice provides a home for freedom precisely insofar as it provides a refuge from the unyielding necessity of natural needs and the biologically determined forces that drive the life process. These forces dominate the household and economic realms, making them sites of inequality (masters and slaves, bosses and employees) and coerced, rather than free, activity.

However, Arendt claims, over the past three centuries we have witnessed "the admission of household and housekeeping activities to the public realm." This takes the form of "social housekeeping" and governmental regulation and oversight of economic activity (*THC*, 45). According to Arendt, there has been an irresistible tendency on the part of society to "grow, to devour the older forms of the political and the private." This constant growth "derives its strength from the fact that through society it is the life process itself which in one form or another has been channeled into the public realm" (*THC*, 45). Here Arendt offers her most concise formulation of what she means by "society" in her discussion of "the rise of the social." Society "is the form in which the fact of mutual dependence for the sake of life and nothing else assumes public significance and where the activities connected with sheer survival are permitted to appear in public" (*THC*, 45).

How did the "fact of mutual dependence for the sake of life and nothing else" assume such an unprecedented *public* significance? Obviously, the expansion of markets, demographic growth, and the commencement of industrialization all played a part in the "rise of the social." But for Arendt the key consequence of the emergence of the modern economy is the way it transformed, in a relatively short time, "all modern communities into societies of laborers and job holders"—that is, into communities "centered around the one activity needed to sustain life," namely, *labor* (*THC*, 46). The fact that we currently live in a society in which an individual's identity is primarily viewed in terms of the kind of job he or she performs (teacher, doctor, construction worker, etc.) can be traced back to this fundamental transformation.

"The moment laboring was liberated from the restrictions imposed by its banishment into the private realm," Arendt writes,

> It was as though the growth element inherent in all organic life had completely overcome and overgrown the processes of decay by which organic life is checked and balanced in nature's household. The social realm, where the life process has established its own public domain, has let loose an unnatural growth, so to speak, of the natural; and it is against this growth, not merely against society but against a constantly growing social realm, that the private and the intimate, on the one hand, and the political (in the narrower sense of the word), on the other, have proved incapable of defending themselves. (*THC*, 47)

The dominant image, then, is that of the huge and complex organism—one born of rapid economic development and the acceleration of society's "life process"—that runs according to the internal imperatives of constant economic growth and ever-increasing technological integration. The public-political realm is reduced to a bureaucratic apparatus whose primary purpose is to administer the regulatory functions necessary to keep the "organic life" of society running as smoothly as possible. Within this "national household" the "communistic fiction" of a unitary macro-subject—Society—becomes all too real, while acting individuals are transformed into "specimens of the animal species mankind" whose behavior is both predictable and conformist. The ultimate and ironic result is that, at the very moment that "the survival of the species could be guaranteed on a world-wide scale," *humanity* finds itself threatened with extinction (*THC*, 46).

Labor, work, and action

Much of Arendt's chapter on "Labor" is devoted to teasing out the reasons why we have come to identify fabrication and the "work of our hands" with the "labor of our bodies." To anticipate: Arendt thinks that the stunning increase in productivity that accompanied the early stages of the industrial revolution was so overwhelming that thinkers as diverse as John Locke, Adam Smith, and Karl Marx were moved to elevate the previously despised activity of labor from the lowest position in the *vita activa*'s hierarchy to the highest. However, the "unprecedented actual productivity of Western mankind" created what Arendt calls an "irresistible tendency to look at all labor as work and to speak of the *animal laborans* in terms much more fitting for *homo faber*" (*THC*, 87). The activity of labor (the production of consumer goods required for the reproduction of human

6. Production of radiators on the assembly line at Ford Motor Company in Detroit, *c*.1920s.

labor-power) was credited with being man's "world-building" capacity, while the activity of work (the process of fabrication, oriented from start to finish by the goal of creating a durable end-product) was viewed as simply another form of labor (Figure 6).

Let's say Arendt is right about this. Why should we be worried by the conflation of two (admittedly somewhat different) types of human activity? What, beyond conceptual clarity, is at stake? The answer has to do with the role this conflation plays in facilitating the "rise of the social" and in undermining the world of durable things that stands between man and nature (the "human artifice"). The elevation of labor in the hierarchy of human activities by Locke, Smith, and Marx is thus no mere curiosity in the history of ideas. Rather, by placing the endlessly recurring cycles of production and consumption at the center of things, this elevation promotes the assimilation of human existence to natural or pseudo-natural processes.

Viewing labor and work as virtually identical undermines what Arendt calls the "thing character of the world," transforming the objects that constitute the human artifice into little more than products or preconditions of the life process. Artifacts that are meant to be lasting (from architecture and the built environment to works of art) come to be viewed in the same terms as consumer goods. They are there to be used up in the course of the life process and then replaced by newer (but equally fungible) versions of themselves.

The erosion of the "thing character of the world" increasingly exposes human existence to the dictates of the life process and direct determination by the rhythms of production and consumption. The tempo of these rhythms is always quickening, thanks to automation and technological improvements. Hence it is that "the danger of future automation is less the much-deplored mechanization and artificialization of natural life than that... all human productivity would be sucked into an enormously intensified life process and would follow automatically, without pain or effort, its ever-recurrent natural cycle." Indeed, "the rhythm of machines would magnify and intensify the natural rhythm of life enormously," not changing but only making more deadly "life's chief character with respect to the world, which is to wear down durability" (*THC*, 132). This fate can be escaped only so long as we are able to maintain a clear distinction between the durable products created by the *work* of the craftsman, artist, or architect (on the one hand) and the fleeting products produced by labor (on the other).

Strictly speaking, the "products" of labor are not really products at all. They lack the relative permanence and objective independence that characterizes the kind of artifacts produced by man in his capacity as fabricator. As *homo faber*, man contributes directly to the creation of the durable thing-world that stands between man and nature. *Without* such a world composed of relatively permanent things, we would find ourselves exposed to the "sublime indifference" of nature itself, subject to an "overwhelming elementary force" that compels us to "swing relentlessly in the circle of [our] own biological movement" (*THC*, 137). As Arendt reminds us,

> The birth and death of human beings are not simple natural occurrences but are related to a world into which single individuals, unique, unexchangeable, and unrepeatable entities, appear and from which they depart. Birth and death presuppose a world which is not in constant movement, but whose durability and relative permanence makes appearance and disappearance possible, which existed before any one individual appeared into it and will survive his eventual departure. Without a world into which men are born and from which they die, there would be nothing but changeless eternal recurrence, the deathless ever-lastingness of the human as of all other animal species. (*THC*, 96–7)

Yet the rise of the social and the "enormously intensified life process" created by automation and the technological integration of the economy appears to be moving us decidedly closer to such a world-less, quasi-naturalized condition.

Arendt thinks the late modern age has come to be defined by attitudes characteristic of the *animal laborans*, for whom life is the greatest good and consumption the greatest happiness. On the other hand, she thinks that the attitudes characteristic of *homo faber* dominated the early modern age, the period when machine technology was just emerging and the "rise of the social" was manifest primarily in the expansion of the division of labor and markets for durable goods. Of course, the human *capacities* for labor, work, and action are all present in the modern age, just as they were in previous epochs. What changes over time is the relative cultural significance of each activity and worldview associated with it. Thus, the narrative arc of *THC* can be said to trace the movement from the cultural hegemony of politics and the life of action in Greece and Rome; to that of fabrication, work, and utility in the early modern age; to the hegemony of labor and the colonization of the public-political realm by the "life process" of society in the present.

THC's chapter on "Work" is important for three reasons. First, it makes clear the difference between "the labor of our bodies" (undertaken for consumption and subsistence) and the "work of our hands" (the fabrication of durable things). Second, it dramatically juxtaposes the worldly quality of *homo faber*'s activity and products to the unworldly quality of the *animal laborans*, whose consciousness and bodily energy are absorbed by the nature-like rhythms of production and consumption. And third, it highlights the contrast between an activity that is repetitive and necessary (labor), and an activity that is determined not by nature, but by the mental picture of the product in the mind of the fabricator (work).

Laboring, an activity dictated by bodily needs, is cyclical and endless, whereas the process of work is linear and finite. It comes to an end in the creation of the finished product, which is an object concretely instantiating the original idea in the mind of the craftsman. This idea not only guides the activity of *homo faber*, it also governs his choice of tools and determines the techniques he employs. The means/end category rules the fabrication process throughout, and it is this fact that gives work its fundamentally instrumental character.

At first glance, Arendt's description of work and the fabrication process appears completely positive, especially when contrasted with the necessity-driven activity of labor. The laborer is effectively the servant of nature, whereas the fabricator is nature's master. The products of work are objective and lasting, constitutive of the artifice that stands between man and nature, whereas those of labor and action are fleeting. The "products" of labor are quickly consumed or used up, while the "products" of action—words and deeds in the public realm—are quickly forgotten unless they are memorialized by the poet, historian, or the political community itself.

However, while the positive quality of work as man's "world-building" capacity is undeniable, *homo faber*'s tendency to generalize the fabrication experience—to look at everything in terms of the means/end category—is inherently problematic. This can be seen at the beginning of the industrial age, which sees the "victory of *homo faber*." Just as the experience of the *animal laborans* dominates the present, leading us to evaluate all things in terms of their contribution to the life process, so the instrumentalizing attitude of *homo faber* dominating the earlier period led to all things being evaluated in terms of their utility. For Arendt, utilitarianism is less a philosophy than a worldview, one that achieved an astonishing hegemony during the 18th century.

The problem is that *homo faber*'s habit of judging a thing in terms of its utility always expands to include the end itself. In any consistent utilitarianism, the "in order to" has a way of becoming the content of the "for the sake of." The prospect of an infinite regress looms, with the value of any given end depending entirely upon its utility for the achievement of some further end. Establishing utility as *the* horizon for the attribution of value leads to the destruction of the inherent worth of any activity or thing and to the generation of meaninglessness (*THC*, 154).

The "victory" of *homo faber*'s utilitarian worldview thus paves the way for the ultimate triumph of the *animal laborans*. The slippery slope represented by the "instrumentalization of the whole world and the earth" can be avoided only so long as the product of work retains its character as a *reification*; that is, only so long as that product remains a "finished object" and is *not* converted into a means to something else (*THC*, 139). However, with the "rise of the social" the prospects for preserving the inherent value of either things or activities become increasingly dim.

The reader will have noticed that, as the analysis of the activities comprising the *vita activa* proceeds, Arendt focuses increasingly on the question of meaning. The activity of labor is cyclical and repetitive, so much so that the *animal laborans* (who produces in order to consume and consumes in order to produce) is ultimately unable to distinguish means from ends. Labor *has* no end since the daily fulfillment of bodily needs can be escaped only in death. In Arendt's view, the cyclical character of labor as an activity makes it incapable of creating any meaning or value that transcends the horizon of organic life.

Work, on the other hand, is *not* determined by the rhythm imposed by nature. *Homo faber* transcends his natural environment, creating a "human artifice" and—with it—a worldly space of intelligibility. Whereas man as *animal laborans* knows only the "eternal recurrence of the same" that attends the material and biological reproduction of the species, man as *homo faber* knows the intentional meaning created by his projects and purposiveness. Yet *homo faber*'s tendency to generalize the fabrication experience—to apply the means/end category not just to specific projects but to the world in general—has the potential to reduce everything to the status of means possessing a merely instrumental value.

It is for this reason that Arendt writes that "*homo faber*, in so far as he is nothing but a fabricator and thinks in no terms but those of means and ends which arise directly out of his work activity, is just as incapable of understanding meaning as the *animal laborans* is incapable of understanding instrumentality" (*THC*, 155). A world structured exclusively in terms of "in order to" and "for the sake of" relationships may be adequate to the task of separating man from nature, but it is incapable of providing what a *human* world should provide: a durable context for non-instrumental meaning, for things and activities that are valuable in themselves. Only a world that provides such a context can, in Arendt's view, be a "home for mortal man."

This is where action enters the picture. Action is, for Arendt, our most distinctively human activity. As the "sharing of words and deeds," action combines the human capacity to begin with the unique revelatory capacity she thinks implicit in speech and deeds that occur on a public stage. It is through public words and deeds that we "insert ourselves into the human world," appearing before our civic peers for the first time and revealing our "unique distinctness":

> This appearance, as distinguished from mere bodily existence, rests on initiative, but it is an initiative from which no human being can refrain and still be human. This is true of no other activity in the *vita activa*. Men can very well live without laboring, they can force others to labor for them, and they can very well decide merely to use

> and enjoy the world of things without themselves adding a single useful object to it; the life of an exploiter or slaveholder and the life of a parasite may be unjust, but they are certainly human. A life without speech and without action, on the other hand... is literally dead to the world; it has ceased to be a human life because it is no longer lived among men. (*THC*, 176)

This is a stunning passage, and it is certainly foreign to the prepossessions of most of us. Can Arendt really mean what she is saying—that a life without political action, without appearing on a public stage, is not a fully *human* life? That our "unique distinctness" as individuals manifests itself not in our psychological quirks or self-expressive activities, but rather in the "words and deeds" performed by our *public* selves? Since Rousseau we have become so used to identifying our *real* selves with our private or inner selves that Arendt's suggestion that the truth lies elsewhere strikes us as wildly implausible.

Arendt is indeed arguing for a critical reexamination of our habitual privileging of the reality of the private or "authentic" over the public or "merely apparent." The cultural roots of this privileging run extraordinarily deep. They go back not just to the Romantics' cult of feeling and sensibility, but to Plato and early Christianity's devaluation of the reality of *this* world (the "cave" of illusory appearances, according to the *Republic*), which they contrast with a "true" or intelligible world that lies beyond the senses (the realm of the Ideas or of God). Arendt's declaration that "for us, appearance—something that is being seen and heard by others as well as ourselves—constitutes reality" (*THC*, 50) is a direct challenge to this privileging. It underscores both her vehement anti-Platonism as well as her hostility to all forms of modern subjectivism, from Descartes to existentialism. She views them all as symptoms of a profound "alienation from the world."

The political actor is, Arendt insists, an *actor*, someone who appears on a public stage and whose medium is opinion (*doxa*) and persuasive speech (*peitho*). The fact that we tend to discount both, viewing the former as an expression of individual sentiment and the latter as rhetorical manipulation, is again due to deeply rooted Platonic-Christian prejudices. It was Plato who instituted the philosophical opposition between a transcendent Truth and all-too-worldly opinion, and it was Catholic Christianity that gave this opposition real social and political power by contrasting God's singular Truth (*Unum Verum*) with multiple forms of illusion and heresy.

Here we must note the difference between a widely shared commitment to factual and rational truths (such as "in 1914 Germany invaded Belgium, and not vice versa" and 2 + 2 = 4) and the partisan desire to impose a philosophically or theologically derived "absolute" truth on the public sphere, one which claims the power to trump all other perspectives and opinions. The former, especially the commitment to factual truth, is a crucial precondition of having a public realm in which "innumerable perspectives" on common objects can appear and be expressed. The latter is a form of what Arendt's contemporary Isaiah Berlin referred to as "monism." This is the assumption that, for every fundamental question in morals and politics (e.g. What is justice? What is the good life?) there must be one and only one correct answer. Monism is the attempt to replace plural opinions and perspectives on such questions with what it considers to be *the* Truth. It is the enemy not only of the public sphere as conceived by Arendt but also of the liberal democratic commitment to tolerance and pluralism.

The fact that *we* treat opinion as something reflexive and pre-rational, the kind of thing polls of public sentiment measure, underlines the degree to which we still labor under the original Platonic/Christian devaluation of *doxa*. For Arendt, as for the democratic Athenians and the American founders, *opinions* are formed through public debate, deliberation, and argument—they are not simply given, like group identities or partisan affiliations.

The more I am able to take the standpoints of others into account, the stronger the arguments supporting my opinion will be, and the more likely I will persuade others to share it. Persuasive speech in the public realm is not the opposite of reasoned argument (as the Platonic distinction between dialectic and rhetoric would have it). It is, rather, one of reasoned argument's most obvious vehicles, even though (or especially because) it does not give us "Truth."

But doesn't Arendt's concern with the *performance* of words and deeds undercut this commitment to rational argument, shifting the focus decisively away from persuasion through reasons to the virtuosity of the political actor? In her essay "What is Freedom?" Arendt herself notes that there is a "strong affinity" between the performing arts and politics, and she describes the *polis* as "a kind of theater where freedom could appear" (*BPF*, 152). If that is indeed the case, then it would seem that the public stage is more suited to the self-aggrandizing gestures of an Alcibiades than to the more somber wisdom of a Pericles or a Lincoln.

This "dramaturgical" view of Arendt on action is surprisingly widespread. However, it rests upon a false dichotomy between the deliberative and performative, and between the agent- and world-disclosive dimensions of action. As Arendt reminds us in the "Action" chapter:

> Action and speech go on between men... and they retain their agent-revealing capacity even if their content is exclusively "objective," concerned with the matters of the world of things in which men move, which physically lies between them and out of which arise their specific, objective, worldly interests. These interests constitute, in the word's most literal significance, something which *inter-est*, which lies between people and therefore can relate and bind them together. Most action and speech is concerned with this in-between, which varies with each group of people, so that most words and deeds are *about* some worldly

objective reality in addition to being a disclosure of the acting and speaking agent. (*THC*, 182)

Plural (equal and distinct) human beings share a common world, but it is through talking about it—through debate, speech-making, and the exchange of opinion about matters that concern all—that they enact their freedom and disclose the meaning(s) of their public world. Of course, this meaning—and the "web of human relationships" that manifests it—is not static or pregiven. It is always "in process," subject not only to events but also to multiple (and often conflicting) interpretations and judgments. Moreover, there can indeed be periods when public speech devolves into ideological sloganeering and "mere chatter," thus lending an at least episodic truth to Heidegger's claim that "the light of the public obscures everything" (*MDT*, ix). But, excepting such "dark times," public-political discourse and the exchange of opinion retain a uniquely illuminative capacity, "lighting up" our common world and the events that shape it.

Self-revelation, then, is hardly the "purpose" of action. It is, however, its invariable accompaniment. What a person says and does in public reveals their identity in a way that transcends the merely personal or psychological. *Who* Pericles and Lincoln were has nothing to do with any inner turmoil or mixed motives they might have had. Rather, their identity is made manifest in their public words and deeds. These are judged and remembered by their peers, and by those who come after. *How* they will be judged and remembered is, of course, not something the actors themselves control. The revelation of who the actor is, occurring through his public speech and actions, takes place within an already existing web of human relationships.

The actor is, in important respects, at the mercy of his "audience" since it is they who interpret, judge, and remember (or forget) his words and deeds. And, of course, his audience is composed by others who are themselves actors, either real or potential.

Their co-presence means that the action initiated by even the most virtuosic of political actors will rarely achieve its original purpose. The actor is also a sufferer, subject not just to the judgments of others but to their "innumerable conflicting wills and intentions" as well (*THC*, 184). Where plurality and equality make themselves felt—where *rulership* and *command* are absent—the consequences of a given action are, in principle, boundless. They ripple out from the original act and intersect with the actions of others, thereby generating unpredictable effects and unforeseeable consequences.

It is precisely this non-sovereign character of action in the public sphere that Western philosophy has generally found intolerable. Arendt argues that, in order to escape action's "frailty, boundlessness, and uncertainty of outcome," our tradition of political thought has consistently reinterpreted action in terms taken from the sphere of fabrication—that is, as a form of *making*. The fabricator begins with an idea or blueprint of the object he wants to create, selects the appropriate means (in the form of tools and raw materials) and—assuming he possesses the requisite "expert wisdom"—*produces* the desired object as a predictable result. In short, *homo faber* rules over the production process from start to finish.

This can hardly be said of the political actor, who must contend with other actors and the "innumerable conflicting wills and intentions" created by the "web of human relationships." However, if citizens could be convinced that the *real* political actor is someone who actually possesses "expert" or craftsman-like moral-political wisdom, then the contingency and unpredictability permeating the public realm could be curbed if not eliminated. In place of the seeming "anarchy" of democratic politics, where there is no ruler and the political actor must act in concert with his peers if what he has initiated is to be carried through, we would have an architectonic politics predicated on a clear separation of those who *know* (the philosophic ruler or statesman who designs and oversees laws and institutions) and those who simply do (the citizen-subjects who obey and carry out his commands). Here the philosophic statesman, the "expert" in matters of virtue and justice, commands and manipulates those he rules in much the same way as the master craftsman shapes his materials and directs his helpers. Viewed in this light, the creation of a just and harmonious political community is dependent upon the presumed reality and availability of such expert moral wisdom, and upon the willingness of citizen-subjects to submit themselves to the authority it supposedly confers.

Readers familiar with Plato will immediately recognize the paradigm created by the *Republic*. In that work, the opinions and speech of plural equals reduce to shadowy illusions. Only he who has detached himself from the realm of human affairs and made the journey to an intelligible realm outside the "cave" of appearances has any chance of gaining true knowledge of virtue and justice. This figure—the philosopher, the lover of wisdom—finds happiness communing with true reality as embodied in the ideal world of the Forms. But, Plato insists, he must be wrenched away from this contemplative idyll and compelled to use his knowledge of the Truth for the benefit of all those still trapped in the cave of conflicting wills and opinions. Armed with political power, the philosopher will do this by "stamping on the plastic matter of human nature in public and in private the patterns he visions there [in the realm of Ideas outside the cave]," molding and fashioning not just himself but the political community as well. He will be, in Plato's words, a "craftsman of sobriety and justice and all forms of ordinary civic virtue" (*Republic*, 500d–501a).

The *Republic* is by far the most famous example of what Arendt calls "the traditional substitution of making for acting," but it is hardly the only one. The imposition of metaphors taken from the realm of fabrication onto politics occurs repeatedly in the Western tradition of political thought, as does the Platonic separation of those who know from those who do. The original harmony of thought and action manifest in a figure like Pericles is sundered and replaced by what Nietzsche called the "fateful distinction" between *theory* and *practice*. Conceived as a tool in the hands of those who know, action apparently ceases to be prey to "frailty, boundlessness, and uncertainty of outcome" and produces, instead, a theoretically predictable (and ostensibly lasting) product: the truly just community.

The Platonic understanding of political action as simply a tool or means to some extra-political end—so foreign to the Greeks, for whom "the sharing of words and deeds" was in many respects the point of life—has long since become an unquestioned presupposition of political discussion, practical as well as theoretical. We are simply unable to think political action outside what Arendt calls the "tyranny of the means/end category." The result has been nothing short of disastrous since the achievement of the "end" implicitly justifies all means.

In denying debate, deliberation, opinion-sharing, and "acting in concert" any value beyond their contribution to the achievement of a pregiven end, we come dangerously close to the idea that what matters is not the preservation of political freedom per se, but the ability of a regime—no matter how authoritarian—to deliver the basic socio-economic goods. Such a stance, aided and abetted by the "rise of the social," clearly undermines our commitment to the democratic practice of politics. It resurrects the distinction between ruler and ruled, governors and governed, potentially transforming us all into subjects of what Tocqueville rightly called an "administrative despotism."

Chapter 4
Revolution, constitution, and the "social question"

Arendt's *On Revolution* (1963) appears to be a much more optimistic book than either *OT* or *THC*. Whereas the earlier volumes dealt with dire threats to the public realm, human plurality, and our capacity for unpredictable ("spontaneous") action, *OR* is a book that celebrates initiatory political action and the possibility of new beginnings. It is, moreover, the most extended piece of writing Arendt did on the nature of *modern* political action. Her beloved Greeks make an appearance, but no one can accuse Arendt of attempting to foist the *polis* model onto either the American or the French Revolution. These are, of course, the two instances of modern revolution that *OR* devotes most of its pages to. They are presented by Arendt as dramatic examples of the human capacity to make new beginnings. They are also manifestations of the kind of "joint action" she thinks ordinary people are capable of, assuming that they are politically organized and not a mere "mass."

While *OR* develops the Arendtian themes of joint and initiatory action in what is clearly a modern context, it also addresses the reasons for the French Revolution's ultimate failure and the (at best) *partial* success of the American Revolution. To argue that the French Revolution "failed" may seem a controversial thesis, but it does have the fact that the First Republic lasted a mere 12 years (from 1792 to 1804) to support it.

Arguing that the American Revolution—a success in terms of establishing a new and durable form of government—failed to preserve the "revolutionary spirit" and *public* freedom is perhaps even more controversial. Her critics have suggested that Arendt has seriously misconstrued the *raison d'être* of American democracy, which is not to provide a space for public freedom but rather to limit government, establish equality under the law, and protect individual rights and liberties. In no small part, this objection is rooted in the standard Lockean-liberal interpretation of the American Revolution, an interpretation which stresses constitutional government, the moral priority of individual rights, the sanctity of property, and the fundamental importance of "negative" liberty (the freedom from interference). *OR* advances what is a robustly republican reinterpretation of the American Revolution, one that has garnered significant historical support in recent decades, notably in books by Bernard Bailyn, Gordon Wood, and J. G. A. Pocock.

Of course, Arendt is fully aware that she is directly contesting the Lockean-liberal account as well as challenging many of our preconceptions about the nature and purpose of American democracy. She wants to remind us of what the founding generation had achieved: the establishment of a completely new, institutionally articulated, "space of freedom," one in which citizens of the republic are provided with the all-important opportunity to become "participators in the government of affairs" (Jefferson). And she wants us to see how the Founders' achievement is obscured by a liberal interpretation that focuses more on individual rights and "free enterprise" than it does on public or political freedom. For this reason alone, it is entirely appropriate to read *OR* as Arendt's "settling of accounts" with the liberal tradition (*CCA*, 220).

Advocates of participatory or "radical" democracy have been among the most fervent admirers of the agonistic or "Greek"

7. Howard Chandler Christy, *Scene at the Signing of the Constitution of the United States* (1940).

theory of political action Arendt advances in *THC*. However, they view her focus on constitutions in *OR* with a good deal of skepticism. They worry that a constitutionally focused politics promotes the "taming" of democracy, dispersing democratic energies while creating barriers to meaningful participation by the *demos* itself. They see constitutionalism as shifting attention away from the all-important *substance* of democracy—the political action of ordinary citizens in the public realm—to formal questions concerning legal process and governmental design.

As we will see, Arendt shares some of these concerns, but—unlike the "radical democrat"—she does not see the American Constitution as a clever bit of engineering designed to limit participation and keep power in the hands of an elite. Rather, she sees it as creating precisely the institutionally articulated "space of freedom" that is at once the most important dimension of the public realm and the framework for substantial political participation by ordinary citizens. While she thinks that the Founders erred in not including the townships as part of their ingenious arrangement of county, state, and federal powers, she does not see them as deliberately setting out to emasculate the democratic potential of their new form of government (Figure 7).

Arendt's constitutional focus in *OR* is perfectly consistent with her earlier emphasis (in *OT*) on the need for durable legal-institutional structures and the importance of a clearly defined public realm (*THC*). The question of how freedom can be given an institutional housing runs like a red thread throughout her work (something we could hardly say of either the Marxist or libertarian traditions). And, while some radical democrats might worry that the resulting constitutional focus undercuts the agonal spirit described in *THC*, for Arendt there is no contradiction. Rather, in the modern era "revolution on the one hand, and constitution and foundation on the other, are like correlative conjunctions" (*OR*, 117). This is so for the simple reason that, "under modern conditions, the act of foundation is identical with the framing of a constitution" (*OR*, 116).

It is only with the framing of a new constitution, with "the establishment of a new body politic, a new form of government," that the "men of the revolutions" on both sides of the Atlantic can be said to have begun an "entirely new story, a story never known or told before." According to Arendt, the "plot" of the story revolved around nothing less than an epoch-making "emergence of freedom" in the West. This was a specifically *political* form of freedom, one that had seemingly disappeared for good with the fall of the Roman Republic (27 BCE). Excepting a few Italian city-states, the intervening centuries had known only rulers and ruled in the political sphere.

Arendt is careful to point out that, at the beginning of their struggles, the 18th-century "men of the revolutions" were scarcely aware of the epochal significance of what they had begun. However, what began with protests directed against particular abuses committed by specific kings quickly and unexpectedly turned into a revolutionary rejection not just of monarchy as a form of government, but of caste hierarchy as an organizing social principle. By the time of the Declaration of Independence (1776) and the abolition of feudal privilege by the National Constituent Assembly (1789), the unique historical significance of their undertakings had become clear to the "men of the revolutions." From that moment forward, they were struck by what Arendt calls the "pathos of novelty," the feeling that nothing remotely comparable to their deeds and accomplishments had ever occurred in the history of the West. The creation of the American and French republics revealed that, by acting together and acting in concert, it was possible for human beings to *interrupt* history—to effect a radical beginning, one that commenced "an entirely new story" that was "never known or told before."

It is this pathos of novelty that Arendt thinks marks the *modernity* of the American and French revolutions. Of course, the ancients were fully aware of the phenomenon of political change, as the histories of Thucydides, Livy, and Polybius all attest. Yet they saw these changes through the lens of a cyclical conception of time, one that assumed that similar situations and events would crop up again and again in history, recurring as endlessly as the seasons. As a result, the ancients lacked the conceptual resources that might have enabled them to grasp the idea of a radical beginning and recognize genuine novelty in the political realm.

While Christianity replaced this cyclical conception of historical time with a fundamentally linear one, the power to begin or interrupt history was reserved for God alone. The unique but transmundane events of the birth of Jesus and the Last Judgment marked the beginning and the end of a new sacred temporality, while in the secular realm the rise and fall of empires continued to be construed in the cyclical manner of the ancients. The idea that men, through acting together, could bring about a genuinely new beginning would have struck such early Christian thinkers as Saint Augustine as blasphemous.

In the modern era, even the so-called "Glorious Revolution" of 1688 in England—the instance of political change that probably loomed largest in the imaginations of the American Founders—was conceived not as a new beginning, but rather as a "revolution back" to a constitutional order that had been disturbed by the absolutist ambitions of the Stuart monarchs. It is only with the American and French revolutions that the modern meaning of the word "revolution" fully emerges. After these events, revolution becomes synonymous with the idea of a radically new beginning in the political world. It comes to signify a transformational political event, one in which "the idea of freedom and the experience of a new beginning... coincide" (*OR*, 19).

The experience of a new beginning is most clearly manifest in the founding of a new republic. Arendt's linkage of revolution to the act of foundation, and foundation with the drawing up of a new constitution, directs us to one of the more counterintuitive arguments to be found in *OR*. Arendt fully acknowledges the fact that a people's struggle for liberation from an oppressor will most likely entail violence. However, she is careful to distinguish such struggles for liberation from revolution proper. The latter is identified with the "new beginning" itself, a beginning that occurs only with the foundation of the republic and the creation of a new form of government.

Making the distinction between *liberation* and a *revolution* properly so called allows Arendt to preserve her earlier distinction (in *THC*) between political action and violence. As we have seen, political action for Arendt is, above all, talkative. In a revolutionary context, political action consists in "the speech-making and decision-taking, the oratory and the business, the thinking and persuading, and the actual doing" that the creation of a new form of government (and a new space of freedom) demand (*OR*, 24). Violence, on the other hand, is mute. It is incapable of disclosing the *meaning* of any given phenomenon. It is for this reason that "political theory has little to say about the phenomenon of violence and must leave its discussion to the technicians" (*OR*, 9).

I should stress that Arendt by no means denies that violence and revolution are often intertwined. Yet it is precisely because we so often conflate the two that we need to clearly distinguish revolution—the most dramatic example of initiatory action to be found in the modern age—from the violent struggle for liberation. The desire for liberation from an oppressor is by no means tantamount to the desire to constitute a new form of government, especially a form of government composed of durable institutions designed to enable "the passion for public freedom" and the "pursuit of public happiness" to receive "free play for generations to come" (*OR*, 117).

But are the "passion for public freedom" and the "pursuit of public happiness" really at the core of revolution properly so-called? Anyone endorsing the liberal-Lockean interpretation of the American Revolution would have to say no. What drives the American Revolution is the desire for government by consent ("no taxation without representation"), limited political power, and the protection of citizens' civil rights—or their "lives, liberties, and properties" in Locke's famous phrase. Yet, as Arendt points out, the liberties spelled out in this formula are "essentially negative." They are "the results of liberation, but they are by no means the actual content of freedom... which is participation in public affairs." Moreover, she states that if revolution had aimed only at the guarantee of civil rights "then it would not have aimed at freedom but at liberation from governments that overstepped their powers and infringed upon old and well-established rights" (*OR*, 22).

Here we encounter what Arendt refers to as the "truly revolutionary element in constitution-making," a radical element born of the Founders' desire for *public* freedom and *public* happiness. Any constitutionally limited form of government, even a monarchy, can in principle preserve and protect the kind of civil rights cherished by the Lockean-liberal tradition. However, only a constitutional republic or democracy can provide the all-important freedom *for* politics, the kind of freedom that enables citizens to become "participators in the government of affairs."

Arendt thinks that it was the desire for this freedom, first felt in the New England townships and subsequently across all the colonies, that determined the Americans' ultimate preference for revolution over reform. In this regard, she—following Tocqueville—contrasts the concrete and nearly 150-year-old experience of local administration and self-governance in the colonies with the abstract yearning of the French *hommes de lettres* for something they themselves had never known: public freedom.

> What was a passion and a "taste" in France was clearly an experience in America, and the American usage which, especially in the eighteenth century, spoke of "public happiness," where the French spoke of public freedom, suggests this difference quite appropriately. The point is that the Americans knew that public freedom consisted in having a share in public business, and that the activities connected with this business by no means constituted a burden but gave those who discharged them in public a feeling of happiness they could acquire nowhere else.... The people went to the town assemblies, as their representatives later were to go to the famous Conventions, neither exclusively because of duty nor, and even less, to serve their own interests but most of all because they enjoyed the discussions, the deliberations, and the making of decisions. (*OR*, 110)

But if the desire to preserve and extend such public happiness drove the colonists to the extremity of revolution, then why doesn't this idea play a larger role in the Founders' thinking and the debates we have from the period leading up to the American Revolution?

The short answer is that it *did* play such a role, but we have been blinded to this fact by Lockean-liberal interpretations of the American Revolution. The longer answer is that the Founders were never entirely clear in their own minds about the difference between public and private happiness. They tended to blur the distinction, formally subordinating public happiness to the pursuit of individual or private happiness. This is one instance where their actions—the struggle for liberation from the "mother" country and the promulgation of a new republican constitution—spoke louder (and more articulately) than their words.

Thomas Jefferson provides a good example in this regard. Jefferson, Arendt notes, worried intensely about the civic corruption that might arise should ordinary citizens be deprived of a "share in public power" and denied any substantive role in the "government of affairs." In this he displayed a thoroughly republican sensibility, one in line with similar concerns expressed by republicans from Tacitus to Machiavelli. Yet Jefferson himself was not entirely clear about the distinction between (and relative ranking of) public and private happiness. This lack of clarity is most glaringly evident in the Declaration's famous assertion that all men have an "unalienable right" to life, liberty, and the pursuit of happiness. However, only two years earlier, in "A Summary View of the Rights of British America, 1774," Jefferson had written of "a right which nature has given all men... of establishing societies, under such laws and regulations as to them shall seem most like to promote *public* happiness" (*OR*, 118).

In Arendt's view, the Declaration's failure to clearly distinguish public freedom and public happiness (on one hand) from the liberty and happiness of the private individual (on the other) had enormous and lasting consequences. For while it is true that, in America, "the foundation of a new body politic succeeded" and "the Revolution achieved its actual end," what Arendt calls the "second task" of the Revolution—assuring the survival of the revolutionary spirit "out of which the act of foundation sprang"—was "frustrated almost from the beginning" (*OR*, 117).

It was frustrated, first, by what Arendt views as the inability of the Founders to acknowledge fully and clearly their own enjoyment of political action and the *bios politikos*. Thus, while John Adams could state that "it is action, not rest, that constitutes our pleasure," and while Jefferson could conclude a letter to Adams by playfully equating "eternal bliss" with "the joys of discourse, of legislation, of transacting business, of persuading and being persuaded" he and Adams had experienced during the revolution, the fact remains that the Christian idea of a *perfecta beatitudo* found not in action but in contemplation continued to outweigh the influence of such worldly or "pagan" ideals (*OR*, 122).

Similarly, the tradition of "lawful monarchical rule" that was part of the colonists' English heritage invariably inclined the Founders (Jefferson included) to articulate their goals more in terms of the negative (or "liberal") freedom *from* politics than in terms of the positive (or republican) freedom *for* politics—the freedom to be a "participator in the government of affairs." Thus, once the genuinely revolutionary moment of the founding of the republic was past, the emphasis

> shifted almost at once from the contents of the Constitution, that is, the creation and partition of power, and the rise of a new realm where, in the words of Madison, "ambition would be checked by ambition"... to the Bill of Rights, which contained the necessary constitutional restraints upon government; it shifted, in other words, from public freedom to civil liberty, or from a share in public affairs for the sake of public happiness to a guarantee that the pursuit of private happiness would be protected and furthered by public power. (*OR*, 126)

The trace of ambiguity that remained in the phrase "the pursuit of happiness" disappeared, and it was henceforth understood "as the right of citizens to pursue their personal interests and thus to act according to the rules of private self-interest" in all spheres. At the same time, the revolutionary idea of constitution-making gave way to a more generic *constitutionalism*. This was an understanding that saw the constitution *not* as an institutional design that employed Montesquieu's "separation of powers" principle to generate *more* power for the new republic, but rather simply as a scheme for limiting the power of government as such. And, as Arendt points out, all non-tyrannical forms of government have been forms of limited government, whether they possessed a written constitution or not.

The "pathos of novelty" that so affected the "men of the revolution" testified to a far more radical—and far more positive—achievement: the creation of government "of the people, by the people, and for the people," in Lincoln's famous phrase. This, and not the idea of constitutionally limited government per se, was what was unprecedented. Arendt thinks that the subsequent American failure to adequately articulate the sheer novelty of the revolutionary enterprise has contributed mightily to the oblivion of both its fundamental experience (the creation of a new space of *political* freedom) and its animating spirit.

With wave upon wave of poor European immigrants coming to America in the late 19th and early 20th centuries, the legacy of public freedom and public happiness receded even further. These immigrants were, understandably, more interested in the possibility of escaping Old World poverty and securing material well-being than they were in becoming republican citizens and "participators in the government of affairs." With the Cold War and the ideological identification of American freedom with the "free enterprise system" in the 1950s, this devolution reaches its nadir.

While the kind of public spirit attested to by Tocqueville has suffered serious decline, the reader of *OR* will be struck less by

Arendt's diagnosis of this decay than by her celebration of the success the American revolutionaries had when it came to the all-important question of creating a new form of government. Indeed, Arendt's enthusiasm for the American *constitutio libertatis* can make one suspect that, as an all-too-grateful European refugee, she suspended her critical faculties when it came to discussing the Constitution of the United States.

This suspicion is heightened by her rather flat verdict regarding the "failure" of the French Revolution. Even the most disenchanted contemporary citizen of the French Fifth Republic would probably find this more than a little mystifying. What, after all, was so great about the American Revolution, and why must the French Revolution be portrayed as failure almost from the start? Moreover, doesn't Arendt herself observe that "nothing could be less fair than to take the success of the American Revolution for granted and to sit in judgment over the failure of the men of the French Revolution" (*OR*, 58)?

To answer these questions, it helps to recall Arendt's description of the pathos of novelty experienced by the "men of the revolutions" as they grappled with the fact that they had, indeed, managed to interrupt history. In both the French and American cases, what started with calls for a reformed or constitutional monarchy quickly transformed itself, in the press of events, into demands for a new polity and the beginning of an entirely new story. As previously mentioned, the "plot" of the story was the "emergence of freedom." This process announced itself with the Declaration of Independence in 1776 and the French abolition of feudal privilege in 1789. The subsequent foundation of the American and French republics (in 1787 and 1792, respectively) gave this emergent freedom a tangible form.

The American Founders never forgot the "plot" of the revolution, nor the need to create durable institutions to preserve this newly emerged freedom. However, their French counterparts were quickly diverted from their original revolutionary-constitutional project. In Arendt's view, it was this failure to carry through on the task at hand—the constitution of liberty in the form of a legally and institutionally articulated public realm open to all citizens—that put the French Revolution on the road to failure. The question, then, is what diverted the French "men of the revolution" from their quintessentially *political* project?

For Arendt, the answer is clear. It was the "social question"—the grinding poverty endured by millions of ordinary French families—that diverted the "men of the revolution" away from their original political project (the constitutional "foundation of freedom") to the vastly more ambitious one of liberating the poor from penury and their enslavement to necessity.

Starting with the fall of the Bastille, multitudes of poor people had flooded the streets of Paris in what seemed a veritable *torrent révolutionnaire*. Driven not by the demand for a new form of government but rather by the far more elemental need for bread, "the multitude rushed to the assistance of the French revolution, inspired it, drove it onward, and eventually sent it to its doom" (*OR*, 50). For once they determined that "a constitution was not a panacea for poverty," the masses "turned against the Constituent Assembly as they had turned against the Court of Louis XVI," seeing in the deliberations of delegates only "a play of make believe, hypocrisy, and bad faith." The *malheureux* "changed into the *enragés*" and violence took the place of debate, deliberation, and decision (*OR*, 100).

Is Arendt blaming the "failure" of the French Revolution on the poor in these and other passages? The answer appears to be yes. This conclusion finds support in the fact that she singles out the absence of poverty in the colonies as one crucial precondition for the political success of the American Revolution. It seems that only countries free of the crushing burden of poverty can have any hope of carrying a *political* revolution to a successful conclusion.

The countries that *do* carry this burden (such as 18th-century France, 20th-century Russia and China, and numerous Latin American nations) are, Arendt implies, doomed to undertake the always violent—and always futile—project of *social* revolution. The latter type of revolution is predicated on the mistaken assumption that violent liberation from the domination of a ruling class will somehow bring an end to poverty. As Arendt points out, this has never happened, for the simple reason that it is impossible to solve the "social question"—the problem of poverty—through violence.

But Arendt is not really blaming the victim here. True, the elemental material needs of the people increasingly take center stage as the French Revolution progresses, to the point where a figure as central as Robespierre could exclaim "*La République? La Monarchie? Je ne connais que la question sociale*" ("The republic? The monarchy? I know only the social question") (*OR*, 46). However, it is less the people themselves (who are indeed driven by "violent and pre-political" needs, the need for bread most of all) than their middle- and upper-class leaders that Arendt indicts. Not subject to the pain and misery of poverty themselves, they could not help but feel both compassion and pity for the suffering multitude.

It was, Arendt argues, this very compassion that led them away from the revolutionary task of creating durable institutions and to attempt a "second" liberation: the liberation of the people not just from tyranny, but from the yoke of necessity (in the form of poverty, hunger, and biological needs) (*OR*, 65). After all, "measured against the immense suffering of the immense majority of the people, the impartiality of justice and law, the application of the same rules to those who sleep in palaces and those who sleep under the bridges of Paris, was like a mockery." But once the revolution opened the gates of the political realm to the poor in Paris and elsewhere, it was "overwhelmed by cares and worries which actually belong in the sphere of the household and which ... could not be solved by political means." Social problems like poverty, hunger, and pressing bodily need are, she insists, actually "matters of administration, to be put in the hands of experts, rather than issues that could be settled by the twofold process of decision and persuasion" (*OR*, 81).

Here we see Arendt developing her distinction between the social and the political in a direction that was bound to frustrate many of her left-leaning admirers. Such frustration, however, pales before the anger they are likely to feel when they first encounter Arendt's analysis of the *destructive* role played by compassion in the French Revolution.

Anyone who cares about the plight of the poor today will more than likely cite lack of compassion as one of the key reasons why we have failed to ameliorate poverty through political and governmental action. The quest for social justice is, among other things, a quest to cultivate compassion for members of our society that extreme poverty has rendered marginal, vulnerable, and effectively rightless. Given Arendt's demonstrated sympathy for the plight of refugees in *OT*, her indictment of compassion and pity in *OR* is bound to come as a bit of a shock. Her critique appears, on the face of it, to be rooted in heartlessness. It also appears to fly in the face of her commitment to "care for the world." How, one might ask, can we care for the world if we fail to care for the most vulnerable in it?

To be clear, Arendt *does* care—she is alive to the pain and humiliation caused by poverty. However, as the passages quoted above indicate, she *doesn't* think the question of poverty can be solved by *political* means—that is, by the "twofold process of decision and persuasion." Rather, it is only through the efficient administrative distribution of things like health care, education, housing, etc. that poverty can be contained if not eliminated. And as we have seen, for Arendt administration is not political. As an activity, it consists in identifying and applying efficient means in order to achieve predetermined policy goals, goals that are not (for whatever reason) the object of end-constitutive debate by a diverse body of citizens in the public realm. Considered as a primary distributor of basic social goods to the least advantaged among us, the modern welfare state has a clear (social) role to play—and it is one that Arendt approves of. However, she does not consider that role *political* since (in her view) in any minimally decent society people will largely agree about the need to provide adequate housing, health care, and education to its members. The vital preconditions of politics—disagreement and a genuine plurality of opinions—are lacking.

At the time of the French Revolution, amelioration of the condition of the poor majority—the provision of the so-called "Rights of the San-culottes" to "dress, food, clothing, and the reproduction of their species"—could scarcely be conceived in terms of social policies designed by experts and implemented by the kind of efficient administration that Bismarck was the first to put in place in Germany in the 1880s. In the late 18th century it could be conceived only in terms of a revolutionary "expropriation of the expropriators"—only, that is, in terms of the confiscation of land, food, and wealth from the over-privileged "first estate" of the Church and the parasitic "second estate" of the aristocracy. The bodily needs of the poor were overwhelming, immediate, violent. It seemed obvious to the more radical wing of the French Revolution (and, later, to Marx) that the means to meet these needs would have to be violent as well.

Hence the revolutionary suspension of basic individual rights, coupled with the seizure of properties and the liquidation of members of the aristocracy and other "counter-revolutionary" elements. As Arendt points out, the extra-legal measures implemented by Robespierre and the Jacobins had no parallel on the American revolutionary scene. In part this was because the massive poverty plaguing the Old World simply did not exist in the American colonies. But it was also due to the American "men of the revolution" remaining focused, from beginning to end, on the strictly political task of creating laws and institutions designed for the promotion of public freedom and public happiness (on the one hand) and the preservation of "lives, liberties, and properties" (on the other).

Confronted by the "immense suffering of the immense majority," the French "men of the revolution" felt compelled to make a special effort at solidarization with the poor, whose dire material conditions they did not share. Following Rousseau, they thought that, by cultivating their own feelings of compassion, they would be able to feel the pain of *le peuple*. Yet, as Arendt points out, real compassion consists in an individual's capacity to share the experience of another's suffering, to be a genuine co-sufferer along with him.

It is obviously impossible for any individual (other, perhaps, than Jesus) to be a co-sufferer with millions, to concretely share the pain of a mass of humanity. However, Robespierre and his fellow Jacobins discovered that transforming the (individual and concrete) *passion* of compassion into the *sentiment* of pity gave them the next best thing: a general and seemingly selfless concern for the misery of *les malheureux*. By thus becoming emotionally "one" with the suffering masses, the "men of the revolution" felt entitled to identify *their* will with the will of the people (*OR*, 65). They could see themselves as faithfully embodying Rousseau's "General Will," that singular popular will that supposedly transcended all selfish interests and that needed neither debate nor deliberation to make itself felt. All it needed was compassionate spokesmen like Robespierre to give it voice.

Like others before her, Arendt traces the links between Rousseau's theory and Robespierre's practice. However, her genealogy is not concerned with the genesis of what the historian J. L. Talmon dubbed "totalitarian democracy." Rather, the essential link for Arendt is between the singularity of the General Will and the somatic oneness of the suffering masses. Where intense bodily need drives the poor into the public realm, and where their self-appointed bourgeois spokesmen respond with a boundless pity born of an evidently selfless moral certitude, there neither opinion nor plurality—the content and precondition of politics, according to Arendt—have any place. Direct action—expropriating the expropriators by whatever means necessary—seems the morally imperative task, its ruthlessness notwithstanding. Not for nothing does Arendt cite a petition submitted by a section of the Parisian Commune to the National Convention: "*Par pitié, par amour pour l'humanité, soyez inhumains!*" ("Out of pity, out of love of humanity, be inhuman!") (*OR*, 79).

With the French Revolution, the poor had become political actors for the first time. Necessity in the form of their sheer bodily needs invaded the public realm, "the only realm where men can be truly free" (*OR*, 50, 104). *Political* revolution—a clear manifestation of man's capacity to make a spontaneous beginning, to interrupt history—increasingly gave way to an idea of a *social* revolution that was driven by forces beyond human control. The biological necessity that propelled the starving masses into the public realm combined with the apparent necessity of History itself.

In Arendt's view, it was Hegel who introduced the idea of History as an all-encompassing, "necessary" process, and with it the notion of a "cunning of Reason" operating behind the backs of the historical actors themselves. And it was Marx's discovery of the dialectical movement of socio-political change (suggested to him by the alternating currents of revolution and counter-revolution in France) that brought the two strands of necessity—one biological, the other historical—together. Out of this synthesis emerged what Arendt calls "the most terrible and, humanly speaking, the least bearable paradox in the whole body of modern thought"—that freedom is the product of necessity and that the two eventually coincide (*OR*, 45).

The contrast here with the American Founders is, Arendt thinks, enormous. "Necessity in motion," whether in the form of a popular *torrent révolutionnaire* or a Hegelian–Marxist historical dialectic, was "entirely absent from the range of experiences of either the American Revolution or American egalitarian society" (*OR*, 103). In contradistinction to the chief actors and analysts of the French Revolution—all of whom had concluded that the Revolution was a force unto itself, a historical movement beyond the control of any of its participants—the sentiment that "man is the master of his destiny, at least with respect to political government" permeated the American revolutionaries (*OR*, 41). Neither the movement of history nor the imperatives of nature could build a "house where freedom can dwell"—only men could. It was the American freedom from the driving forces of bodily want and any notion of historical necessity that enabled the "men of the revolution" to maintain a strict and unvarying focus upon the revolutionary task at hand: the "constitution of liberty" by means of a written constitution to be ratified by all the colonies.

But while Arendt writes glowingly about the "superior wisdom" of the American Founders, she does not give them an uncritical pass. She is careful to note their structural advantage insofar as there were "no overwhelmingly urgent needs that would have tempted them to submit to necessity, no pity to lead them astray from reason" (*OR*, 85). Indeed, she thinks that one reason why the French Revolution, rather than the American, became *the* paradigm for virtually all subsequent revolutions is that the American Revolution took place in a kind of "ivory tower"—that is, under circumstances that enabled its chief protagonists to remain blissfully unacquainted with the "social question." Such conditions were and are exceedingly rare in human history. Moreover, she observes that American thinkers have been notably deficient in remembering, preserving, and theorizing the fundamental experiences—including public freedom, public happiness, and public spirit—underlying the Revolution. It is this deficiency, she thinks, which has facilitated forgetfulness of the "revolutionary spirit" and the substitution of market freedom for genuine (public and political) freedom.

But neither their material advantages, nor the failure of subsequent generations to remember the experiences underlying the revolution, are things for which the Founders can be blamed. What they *can* be blamed for, however, is their failure to provide constitutionally rooted spaces for local political participation of the sort previously provided by the townships. Jefferson was keenly aware that the staggered governmental arrangement of federal, state, county, and municipal powers left out the grass roots level of political life. Without some institutional space provided for participation at that level, Jefferson feared that the political involvement of citizens would be limited to elections. This lack of active involvement would cement the hegemony of private interests over public spirit among citizens while creating an "elective despotism" in the form of representatives and government officials ruling over a passive electorate: "If once [our people] become inattentive to public affairs, you and I, and Congress and Assemblies, Judges and Governors, shall all become wolves" (Jefferson, quoted in *OR*, 230).

To prevent this from happening, and to prevent the spread of privatism and civic corruption among citizens, Jefferson advocated dividing the counties into wards. This was a stop gap solution to the constitution's notable failure to incorporate the townships into its system of power: "He [Jefferson] expected the wards to permit the citizens to continue to do what they had been able to do during the years of the revolution, namely, to act on their own and thus to participate in public business as it was transacted from day to day" (*OR*, 243). This scheme, however, never came to fruition, and what Arendt calls the "fateful failure" of the Founders to "incorporate and duly constitute" the townships amounted to a "death sentence" for them and for the very town-hall meetings where ordinary citizens had, for well over a century, participated in public affairs. Hence the paradoxical legacy of the American Revolution: "it was in fact under the impact of the Revolution [and the *constitutio libertatis*] that the revolutionary spirit in America began to wither away, and it was the Constitution itself, this greatest possession of the American people, which eventually cheated them of their proudest possession" (*OR*, 231).

The idea that "preservation of the revolutionary spirit" should be the criterion of the relative success or failure of the American Revolution seems counterintuitive. The 18th-century notions of public freedom and public happiness cited by Arendt are far removed from everyday life in the 21st. Nevertheless, she does have a point. Our domestic politics has long been a politics of interest groups, one in which corporate donations and lobbyists provide monied interests privileged access to the public realm. Ordinary citizens, on the other hand, find themselves increasingly shut out of the public realm and the deliberation and decision that occur within it. If we add to this diminished access the antipolitical effects of consumer culture, there seems no escaping the conclusion that we are "corrupt," at least according to the civic republican definition of this term.

If the "social question" and the "Rights of the Sans-Culottes" sent the French Revolution to its doom, and if the unchecked growth of interest group politics has helped to create a "de facto oligarchy" and permanent state of civic corruption in the United States, then one might conclude that the revolutionary spirit Arendt prizes is less a "lost treasure" than an oasis-like apparition, one that led a fugitive existence even in the age of revolution. Arendt's response to such skepticism is to point to the council system, a system of government that emerged spontaneously from the very workers' and soldiers' councils that had played a leading role in many of the European revolutions that occurred after 1848.

The councils were "always organs of order as much as organs of action." Nevertheless, they were undoubtedly "spaces of freedom"

(*OR*, 256). In addition to their repudiation of the traditional parliamentary parties (composed of elites), they stood in direct opposition to revolutionary parties led by "professional revolutionaries" such as Lenin. Arendt describes the aim of the councils:

> Far from wishing to make the revolution permanent, their explicitly expressed goal was to "lay the foundations of a republic acclaimed in all its consequences, the only government which will close forever the era of invasions and civil wars"; no paradise on earth, no classless society, no dream of socialist or communist fraternity, but the establishment of the "true Republic" was the reward hoped for as the end of the struggle. And what had been true in Paris in 1871 remained true for Russia in 1905, when the "not merely destructive but constructive" intentions of the first soviets were so manifest that contemporary witnesses "could sense the emergence and the formation of a force which one day might be able to effect the transformation of the State." (*OR*, 256)

What impresses Arendt about the council system is the way its episodic appearance testifies to the political instincts and abilities of ordinary people who find themselves living in extraordinary (revolutionary) times. Over the last two centuries, the council system has repeatedly emerged at moments of crisis when the all-powerful sovereign state had collapsed. True, it did not last long in any of the historical instances Arendt cites (the Paris Commune of 1870; the widespread strikes in 1905 and the 1917 February Revolution in Russia; the German Revolution of 1918–19; and the Hungarian revolt of 1956). Nor did many of the workers' councils "clearly distinguish between participation in public affairs and *administration* or *management* of things in the public interest" (*OR*, 266, my emphasis). Yet despite their lack of durability and their tendency to conflate political participation with managerial tasks, the councils *did* provide spaces of freedom where all had the opportunity to "participate in the governing of affairs," at least in principle.

This is what counts for Arendt: the councils' creation of an accessible public space of freedom, one not dominated by vested interests or party elites, nor monopolized by a ruler or ruling class. Perhaps most astonishingly, during the February Revolution of 1917 and the Hungarian revolt of 1956 the system spontaneously generated its own federative structure in the form of a graduated pyramid of councils:

> The most striking aspect of these spontaneous developments is that in both instances it took these independent and highly disparate organs no more than a few weeks, in the case of Russia, or a few days, in the case of Hungary, to begin a process of co-ordination and integration through the formation of higher councils of a regional or provincial character, from which finally the delegates to an assembly representing the whole country could be chosen. As in the case of the early covenants, "cosociations," and confederations in the colonial history of North America, we see here how the federal principle, the principle of league and alliance among separate units, arises out of the elementary conditions of action itself... The common object was the foundation of a new body politic, a new type of republican government which would rest on "elementary republics" in such a way that its own central power did not deprive the constituent bodies of their original power to constitute. (*OR*, 259)

Of course, the federative principle was discovered by the American Founders as well, who applied Montesquieu's "separation of powers" doctrine in a way that produced what Arendt calls "the greatest American innovation in politics," namely, "the consistent abolition of sovereignty within the body of the republic" (*OR*, 144). The council system achieved the same end, creating an integrated structure of plural constituent bodies where before there had been a centralized sovereign state. Both can be said to have effected a "transformation of the state" and created a "new form of government."

The Americans, however, preserved a plurality of constituent bodies (states, counties, etc.) while sacrificing the spaces of local political participation—the townships—that had been the "engine" of the revolution. The council system did not make the same mistake, maintaining from start to finish the contribution and integrity of the most local "spaces of freedom." Yet unlike the American constitutional order, the councils were quickly undone by revolutionary political parties (Russia in 1917) or counter-revolution (Germany in 1918–19). Hence Arendt's epitaph for the radical possibility represented by the recurrent yet all-too-fleeting appearance of the council system: "It was nothing more or less than this hope for a transformation of the state, a new form of government that would permit every member of the modern egalitarian society to become a 'participator' in public affairs, that was buried in the disasters of the twentieth-century revolutions" (*OR*, 256–7).

Chapter 5
Judging, thinking, and willing

In Chapter 1 I described how, in 1961, Arendt came to attend the trial of SS Lt. Colonel Adolf Eichmann in Jerusalem and how the encounter with Eichmann "in the flesh" disconcerted her. Like many others in the trial audience, she expected to be confronted with a virulently anti-Semitic Nazi, one who might try to minimize participation in crimes against humanity by claiming he was "only following orders," but whose commitment to the "Final Solution" would be clear. Instead, she found herself confronted by an individual whose "manifest shallowness" made it "impossible to trace the uncontestable evil of his deeds to any deeper level of roots or motives." "The deeds were monstrous, but the doer…was quite ordinary, commonplace, and neither demonic nor monstrous" (*LM*, 4). It was Eichmann's very ordinariness that led her to cite him as an example of what she famously called "the banality of evil" (Figure 8).

In coining this phrase, Arendt was not suggesting that evil is banal. Rather, her point was that the worst crime we can think of—the Nazi extermination of European Jewry—depended not simply upon the ideologically motivated architects of genocide such as Hitler, Himmler, and Reinhard Heydrich, but also many "normal" individuals who viewed themselves as implementing policy and doing their jobs.

8. War crimes trial of Adolf Eichmann, Jerusalem, Israel, 1961.

As a general point, this is no doubt a valid one. And it applies not just to "desk murderers" (like Eichmann) but even to some of the "foot soldiers" of the Holocaust (well documented in Christopher Browning's book *Ordinary Men*). Whether Arendt was totally correct with respect to Eichmann himself has been a matter of dispute, with some claiming that Eichmann "performed" the role of an unimaginative and not particularly bright bureaucrat at his trial, precisely to undercut the prosecution's attempt to establish the *mens rea* (criminal intent) necessary for a guilty verdict.

In the present context, however, the question is not whether Arendt was right about Eichmann per se, but rather how she went about forming her judgment in the first place. Here we must note that the "banality of evil" was not a familiar phrase prior to Arendt's formulating it. This is important. It shows that Arendt, when confronted with a concrete *particular* (Eichmann in the flesh), found herself unable to place him under the ready-to-hand concepts (or descriptive "universals") that she and others had brought to the trial, "fanatical SS man" and "vicious anti-Semite" chief among them. Arendt, in other words, had to search for a concept adequate to the "new type of criminal" she felt Eichmann represented.

Arendt's judgment of Eichmann is thus a perfect example of what Kant described as "reflective judgment." In his *Critique of Judgment*, Kant states that "judgment in general is the faculty of thinking the particular as contained under a universal." If this was all there was to it, our faculty of judgment would amount to little more than the ability to subsume a variety of particulars under appropriate general concepts ("Socrates is a man," "Fido is a dog," etc.). But, as Kant points out, that is not all there is to it. Judgment as the ability to subsume particulars (what Kant calls "determinative judgment") applies to those cases where "the universal" (the appropriate concept: man, dog, etc.) is "given." However, in addition to such easy cases we are sometimes confronted by instances where "only the particular is given" and the appropriate universal concept is lacking (or, at least, far from obvious). At such moments, we cannot "descend" from the relevant pregiven concept to the particular instance; rather, we have to "ascend" from the particular to a by no means obvious universal concept. The latter becomes something we must either actively uncover or imaginatively invent (*CJ*, 18).

Considered abstractly, Eichmann was a ruthless SS man and (more than likely) a vicious anti-Semite. However, considered concretely, Eichmann's very ordinariness and evident lack of "base motives" marked him as something else entirely. Hence Arendt's coinage of the concept of "the banality of evil." This is the kind of evil we confront whenever a governmental bureaucracy, working in tandem with police and the military authorities, implement criminal policies (ranging from mass deportation to genocide) that the regime has labelled legal and legitimate. In such instances, it is entirely possible that the "new type of criminal" commits his crimes "under circumstances that make it well-nigh impossible for him to know or feel that he is doing wrong" (*EJ*, 276).

At his trial, Eichmann quickly adapted to the norms and understandings underpinning Israeli law, and readily acknowledged the "Final Solution" as one of the worst crimes in human history. However, Eichmann also insisted that his activities in pursuit of this "solution" were *not* criminal at the time he performed them. Indeed, he made a point of insisting that he had not only "followed orders," he had *obeyed the law*. And, since the legal system of the Third Reich was based upon a command theory of law, one in which the Führer's word had the force of law, he had a point (*EJ*, 135).

We find it hard to believe that Eichmann's conscience was quieted solely by the legal status of his duties (his view of himself as first and foremost a "law-abiding citizen" notwithstanding). Indeed, other factors were involved. Chief among them was Eichmann's participation in the Wannsee Conference organized by his superior, Reinhard Heydrich, in January 1942. It was in the Berlin suburb of Wannsee that Heydrich revealed the regime's plans for the Final Solution to assorted undersecretaries of state. These 13 men represented various ministries (the Foreign Office, the Ministry of Justice, the Ministry of the Interior, etc.) whose cooperation would be critical if Europe was to be "cleansed" of Jews.

Both Heydrich and Eichmann expected the undersecretaries to respond with reluctance if not outright protest at the new policy. To their considerable surprise, the proposal was met with universal enthusiasm. Confronted by the total approbation expressed by these "high personages," Eichmann—who had harbored doubts about "such a bloody solution through violence"—experienced what he described as a "Pontius Pilate moment." During his interrogation by Israeli police, he stated that "here now, during this conference, the most prominent people had spoken, the Popes of the Third Reich... At that moment... I felt free of all guilt" (*EJ*, 114).

Eichmann's conscience was quieted, in large part, by the fact that the Final Solution had been endorsed by men who far outranked him and who were, indeed, his "social betters." If they saw nothing wrong with the policy, why should he? But his conscience was also quieted by the fact that, as he went about drawing up schedules of organizing "shipments" of Jews to the death camps, he never encountered anyone who "came to me and reproached me for anything in the performance of my duties," either among the councils of "Jewish Elders" he regularly dealt with or among the few Christian clerics who came to him seeking better treatment for the Jews. A notable example of the latter was Protestant Pastor Heinrich Gruber, who was a witness at the trial. Gruber had personally pleaded with Eichmann for more humane treatment of the Jews. However, he did so on behalf of Jewish World War I veterans and their widows, categories which the Nazis themselves had recognized as special cases. As Eichmann himself put it at the trial, "He [Gruber] came to me and sought alleviation from suffering but did not actually object to the very performance of my duties as such" (*EJ*, 131). Indeed, Gruber tacitly acknowledged the legitimacy of the general rule under which Eichmann operated.

In short, Eichmann encountered no one who actually questioned the legitimacy of the Final Solution as policy. This is important, since when Arendt describes Eichmann as "thoughtless" in *EJ*, she is not implying that he was stupid or slow-witted. Rather, she is pointing to a total lack of reflection on any of the policies or practices he was tasked to implement. His reliance on bureaucratese, stock phrases, and clichés insulated him from the horrific realities of his job, realities we—like the judges in Jerusalem—assume must have troubled his conscience (TMC, 160). Arendt's description of Eichmann as "thoughtless" also points to his marked inability to see things from the standpoint of others—this despite his regular contact with the "Jewish Elders" (who comprised the "Jewish Councils" the Nazis charged with keeping order in the ghettoes) and the fact that he had seen with his own eyes what "deportation for special treatment" really meant when he personally visited Treblinka, Chelmno, and Minsk (*EJ*, 88).

Reflecting on her experience at the Eichmann trial, Arendt wrote in 1971 that it was "this total absence of thinking" that attracted her attention, and which led her to ask the following questions:

> Is wickedness, however we may define it... *not* a necessary condition for evildoing? Is our ability to judge, to tell right from wrong, beautiful from ugly, dependent upon our faculty of thought? Do the inability to think and a disastrous failure of what we commonly call conscience coincide? The question that imposed itself was, could the activity of thinking as such, the habit of examining and reflecting upon whatever happens to come to pass... be of such a nature that it "conditions" men against evildoing? (TMC, 160)

At first glance, Arendt's suggestion seems predictable, even trite. After all, nothing is more common in the Western tradition than philosophers claiming that the philosophical life is the best or most virtuous life, and that philosophical thinking is the path to objective knowledge of the Good. However, Arendt is not Plato or Aristotle. In direct contrast to their view of thinking as a specialized art practiced only by a philosophical few, she forthrightly asserts that if the ability to tell right from wrong has anything to do with the ability to think, then "we must be able to 'demand' its exercise in every sane person no matter how erudite or ignorant, how intelligent or stupid he may prove to be" (TMC, 164). Thinking as Arendt conceives it is a type of reflection that we are all capable of, provided we take the time to "stop and think" and engage in a questioning inner dialogue with ourselves.

To illustrate her point, Arendt puts forward a "model thinker," Socrates. Her choice of model appears to undermine the distinction Arendt wishes to make between thinking as a form of reflection available to all and thinking as conceived by the Western philosophical tradition. Yet, according to Arendt, Socrates is no Plato or Aristotle. He does not pretend to have certain knowledge of what the "Good" is, nor a confident grasp of what the virtues are and how they are to be practiced. As the more "Socratic" Platonic dialogues attest, Socrates has questions, not answers. He knows what he does not know. That is one reason why he finds concepts such as courage, piety, and justice thought-provoking. If Socrates knew the "correct" definitions of these concepts he would have no reason to examine them. Nor would he be driven to annoy his fellow Athenians with endless questioning about such basic and seemingly self-evident moral terms.

Socratic questioning, in the form of *elenchus* or cross-examination, does not yield answers. Rather, it undermines the falsely confident understandings Socrates encounters among his interlocutors, whether these be ordinary citizens or educated sophists. Arendt realizes that her focus on the negative or dissolvent side of Socratic rationality will provoke an obvious objection: if you spend your time undermining the conventional understanding of piety, then it's entirely possible your interlocutors will come away thinking a life of impiety is preferable. Given the trajectory of Socrates' most famous "student," Alcibiades, this objection is not without weight.

Arendt, however, does not flinch from the charge that the kind of thinking she finds in Socrates is "dangerous." Quite the contrary, she embraces it. Thinking is dangerous insofar as the activity of critical examination, in revealing hidden implications and tacit assumptions, hypothetically negates accepted opinions and values. Insofar as it is critical—and for Arendt, as for Socrates, all genuine thinking *is* critical—it is a "resultless enterprise," leaving us with questions and perplexities, but not answers.

How, then, does thinking as reflection—this "dangerous and resultless enterprise"—help to "condition" men against evildoing? Arendt's answer is twofold. First, subjecting a society's reigning table of values to critical examination uncovers the prejudgments undergirding many widely shared (or "conventional") opinions. Socratic cross-examination reveals the built-in contradictions and unthought implications of these opinions, but not merely to facilitate a more consistent reformulation. Rather, what Arendt calls the "purging element in thinking" reveals the implications of unexamined opinions "and thereby destroys them" (TMC, 188). The intrinsically destructive character of all genuine thinking has, according to Arendt, "a liberating effect on another human faculty, the faculty of judgment, which one may call, with some justification, the most political of man's mental abilities" (TMC, 188). For judgment is liberated only to the extent that we can free ourselves from received opinion and preconceived categories.

Second, the activity of thinking—the silent dialogue between me and myself that occurs when I reflect and think something through—cultivates what Arendt refers to as our inner plurality. The habit of thought acquaints each of us with an internal "thinking partner," another self with whom we must try to come to agreement. It is this inner plurality that Socrates appeals to when, in the *Gorgias*, he states, "It would be better for me that my lyre or a chorus I directed should be out of tune and loud with discord, and that multitudes of men should disagree with me rather than that I, being one, should be out of tune with myself and contradict me" (*Gorgias*, 82c). For Arendt, Socrates' fear of disagreeing with himself, of being out of tune with a "thinking partner" he can never escape, provides the basis for a secular conscience, a conscience that does not present itself as the "voice of God in man."

Arendt ties these two aspects together in the conclusion to her essay, making clear the relation she sees between the activity of thinking and "moral considerations":

> If thinking, the two-in-one of the soundless dialogue, actualizes the difference within our identity as given in consciousness and thereby results in conscience as its by-product, then judging, the by-product of the liberating effect of thinking, realizes thinking, making it manifest in the world of appearances where I am never alone and always much too busy to be able to think. The manifestation of the wind of thought is no knowledge; it is the ability to tell right from wrong, beautiful from ugly. And this indeed may prevent catastrophes, at least for myself, in the rare moments when the chips are down. (TMC, 189)

In "emergency situations" where "everybody else is swept away unthinkingly" (like Nazi Germany) thinking "ceases to be a marginal affair" and becomes "political by implication." Indeed, Arendt goes so far as to call it "a kind of action" in such contexts. However, it is a kind of action only in the sense that the individual who thinks and judges for himself is less likely to be party to injustice and evil as policy.

But what about less extreme situations, situations where not everyone has been "swept away unthinkingly" and where publicly articulating a moral or political judgment does not result in a prison term or death sentence?

When discussing political and moral judgment, many political theorists turn to Aristotle's discussion in the *Nicomachean Ethics*. Aristotle's treatment of judgment is appealing because he strongly distinguishes between the prudence that informs good judgment (on the one hand) and scientific or technical knowledge (on the other). Knowing the right thing to do in a particular set of circumstances depends on the ability to "deliberate well" about moral and political matters. Such "practical wisdom" cannot be reduced to a method or a teachable subject matter. The man of good judgment, the *phronimos*, is one with wide experience, good character, and exceptional deliberative ability. He is, however, something of an exception—more of a "statesman" than an ordinary citizen.

It is not entirely surprising, then, that Arendt, while appreciative of Aristotle's discussion, found herself drawn to the conception of judgment Kant offers in the third *Critique*. His focus on *aesthetic* judgment notwithstanding, Kant's conception is attractive to Arendt for three main reasons. First, unlike Aristotle, he is committed to equality and thinks that we all possess a faculty of judgment and the capacity to form reflective judgments (even though we may often fail to utilize it). Second, Kant's focus on aesthetic judgment leads him to place emphasis on shared *appearances* and the judgment of *particulars* (*this* is beautiful, *this* is ugly, etc.). This accords with Arendt's view of what we are in fact doing when we judge specific (commonly perceived) actions and events in the realm of human affairs. Third, Arendt is attracted to Kant because of the stress he places upon the *intersubjective* nature of judgments of taste, a dimension that is (at best) only implicit in Aristotle.

Arendt sees the intersubjective dimension of taste judgments as fundamental:

> The power of judgment rests on a potential agreement with others, and the thinking process which is active in judging something is

> not, like the thought process of pure reasoning, a dialogue between me and myself, but finds itself always and primarily, even if I am quite alone in making up my mind, in an anticipated communication with others with whom I know I must finally come to some agreement. From this potential agreement judgment derives its specific validity. (*BPF*, 217)

The "specific validity" of both political and taste judgments depends on two factors. First, I must be able to eliminate all that is merely subjective or idiosyncratic from my judgment; otherwise, it will have little chance of gaining assent from others in the public realm. My ability to do this depends upon the cultivation of what Arendt, following Kant, calls an "enlarged mentality." This is "the ability to see things not only from one's own point of view but in the perspective of all those who happen to be present" (*BPF*, 218). This ability is closely related to my capacity for "representative thinking." The latter is the imaginative capacity to re-present the views of others when I am alone and in the process of forming an opinion or judgment. If I am unable to train my imagination to "go visiting" the viewpoints of others then it is unlikely that my judgment will be free of subjective or idiosyncratic elements, let alone escape the straitjacket of ingrained prejudices or ideological reflexes.

The second factor is the judging individual's familiarity with, and capacity for, deliberative and persuasive speech. Unlike factual statements (which are empirically verifiable) or rationally demonstrable propositions, the validity of judgments in the moral, political, and aesthetic spheres is redeemed through persuasion and the giving of reasons to one's judging peers. This is the primary similarity between judgments of taste (as analyzed by Kant) and political judgments. As Arendt puts it, taste judgments "share with political opinions that they are persuasive; the judging person—as Kant says quite beautifully—can only 'woo the consent of everyone else' in the hope of coming to an agreement with him eventually" (*BPF*, 219).

The idea that political relations are expressed through persuasive speech and inhabit the realm of opinion has been one that political rationalists and theocrats have long found intolerable. The philosopher-king, the vanguard party, the medieval Church, and the politicized evangelical are all convinced that they possess the "Truth," and that only a polity based on this truth can ever claim to be genuinely just. None of them shrink from the fact that realizing their idea of a "just" society would radically undercut human plurality and curtail if not eliminate plurality of opinion. These two phenomena—the constitutive conditions of politics as Arendt understands it—are attacked as sources of relativism and moral corruption. In the eyes of political rationalists and theocrats, moral and political judgment is the monopoly of the privileged few who *know* what Reason, Nature, or God commands, and who think that all worldly phenomena can be easily subsumed under the categories and principles that have been vouchsafed to them.

The Life of the Mind

In the introduction to *The Life of the Mind* Arendt relates how, in Jerusalem, she was struck not by Eichmann's ideological convictions (which were formulaic) but by his "thoughtlessness." It was this absence of reflection that leads Arendt to ask, "is wickedness... *not* a necessary condition for evil-doing? Might the problem of good and evil, our faculty of telling right from wrong, be connected with our faculty of thought?" (*LM*, 5)

Coming, as it does, at the beginning of a work whose first volume is devoted to the mental activity of thinking, the reader might well assume that Arendt has turned from what she called "the problem of Action" to the "life of the mind" because she wanted to follow up this suggestion and demonstrate how our faculty of thought and what we commonly call conscience are internally linked. That, however, is not her purpose. To frame the mental activity of thinking as, simply, an element necessary for an *active* conscience is to deny that it has any value of its own. The significance of the "habit of reflection" would be reduced to its possible contribution to a *moral* end. This is *not* what Arendt wants to do. Just as she probed the intrinsic significance of political action and participation in *THC*, so (in *LM*) Arendt wants to probe the nature and significance of thinking *as an activity*, distinct from whatever "by-products" it may create—even a by-product as important as conscience and the ability to tell right from wrong.

Does this mean that in *LM* Arendt is abandoning her abiding concern with the *vita activa* for the *vita contemplativa* and what Boethius called "the consolations of philosophy"? The answer is no. Thinking is, for Arendt, essentially an *activity*, whereas contemplation—the "beholding of the Truth" that is the lodestar of Greek philosophy and Christian theology—is a *passivity*, an openness to Being or the Divine that happens only with the cessation of *all* activity and the attainment of complete stillness. Arendt had concluded *THC* with a quotation from Cato: "Never is he more active than when he does nothing, never is he less alone than when he is by himself" (*THC*, 325). In *LM*, as in *TMC*, she underlines the accuracy of this description of thinking as an activity by once again turning to her model thinker, Socrates.

The portrait of Socrates in *LM* contains many of the elements Arendt attributed to him in TMC. However, there is one notable difference. Whereas in TMC the emphasis was on how Socrates' inner plurality lays the groundwork for a secular conscience, in *LM* the focus is on the nature of Socrates' "passionate thinking" itself.

Socratic thinking is essentially negative and dissolvent. It begins with the perplexity Socrates himself experiences when confronted by such basic moral concepts as courage, justice, and piety. These concepts, effectively "frozen" by the conventional definitions, are singularly thought-provoking to Socrates, prompting an "inward dialogue carried on by mind with itself" (*Sophist*, 263e). In the words of the *Theaetetus*, "when the mind is thinking it is simply talking to itself, asking questions and answering them" (189e). The inner dialogue of the thinking activity is profoundly restless. It constantly alternates between moving forward and then retracing its own steps and beginning again. Thus, the "examined life" manifest in such thinking is, in certain respects, as contrary to the contemplative ideal as the *vita activa* itself.

The inner dialogue of thinking—what Arendt calls the "soundless dialogue between me and myself"—provides the model for the dialogical encounters we find in Plato's Socratic dialogues. Here Socrates can be seen *performing* thinking, precisely by means of questioning and relentlessly cross-examining his interlocutors. And, just as reflecting on something doesn't dissolve all our perplexities, so the dialogues themselves produce no final or "correct" definition of the concept in question. Viewed from this angle, the Socratic dialogues support Arendt's contention that the mental processes involved in reflection are neither essentially cognitive nor technical in character. She cites Heidegger: "Thinking does not bring knowledge as do the sciences. Thinking does not produce usable practical wisdom. Thinking does not solve the riddles of the universe. Thinking does not endow us directly with the power to act."

Why, then, do we think? More to the point, what makes us think? Here Arendt contrasts Socrates' answer to that of Plato and the Roman Stoics. In another passage from the *Theaetetus* (155d), Plato has Socrates' interlocutor Theaetetus admit that he has been left "wondering" by the various puzzles the philosopher has adduced concerning the relativity of sense perceptions. Plato's Socrates responds in a surprisingly positive manner to Theaetetus' disorientation and "wondering":

> For this is chiefly the passion (*pathos*) of the philosopher, to wonder (*thaumazein*). There is no other beginning and principle (*archē*) of philosophy than this one. And I think he [Hesiod] was not a bad

genealogist when he made Iris [the Rainbow and messenger of the gods] the daughter of Thaumas [the Wonderer].

The Platonic idea that philosophy begins in wonder—repeated by Aristotle in his *Metaphysics*—became canonical for the entire Western tradition. But what arouses the philosopher's admiring wonder? Not, according to Arendt, the beauty of appearances or the glory of "great words and deeds" immortalized by Homer and other pre-philosophic Greeks. Rather, what aroused the philosophers' admiring wonder was the hidden and harmonious order supposedly behind the "sum total of the things of the world" (*LM*, I, 143).

Philosophy begins, then, with "an awareness of this invisible order of the *kosmos*." It is only by turning away from the realm of the senses and the *vita activa* that the philosopher can hope to attain the stillness necessary to commune with this order. The primary value of *philosophical* thinking for the tradition is that it removes the individual from the buzz of the sensible world, enabling him to develop his purely intellectual powers through the exercise of sophisticated forms of abstraction. Reasoning detached from the senses and empirically based cognition opens what Plato (in Bk. VII of the *Republic*) referred to as eyes of the mind, eyes prepared for "seeing" the intelligible and immutable reality *behind* appearances. The chief virtue of the "dialogue of me with myself," then, is not that it cultivates the habit of reflection on worldly events or things. Rather, it is that it prepares one for a contemplative communion with the order (or truth) of Being. Thinking as an activity is, from this perspective, the ladder the philosopher must climb to attain the detachment, the quiet of mind and soul, necessary to "behold" the Truth.

A quite different answer to the question of "what makes us think?" is found in the Roman Stoics. Wonder at Being no longer prompts thinking. Rather, it is the desire to escape a harsh worldly reality, one in which torture and violent death are all too common. The

Stoics discovered that by giving priority to the contents of our consciousness we can relativize and even deny the reality of the external world as well as the pain and suffering it causes. I may be roasting inside the Phalaric bull but I can still be happy, since I know that the reality of the pain I suffer reduces to nothing more than my conscious perceptions. And over these I remain sovereign.

The Socratic answer to the question "what makes us think?" is decidedly different from either the Platonic or Stoic ones. It is not, however, the one we might expect from *reading* TMC or Plato's *Apology of Socrates*. Both texts imply that Socrates' thinking and questioning are subordinate to a *moral* end: the avoidance of injustice. But if that were the case, then thinking and the habit of reflection would possess, at best, an instrumental value. However, when Socrates in the *Apology* states that the unexamined life is not worth living, he does so not because he fears that leading an unexamined life will lead to Eichmann-like complicity with evil. According to Arendt, he makes this statement because a life without thinking cannot be said to be fully alive. For Socrates, "there is no ulterior motive or ulterior purpose for the whole enterprise. An unexamined life is not worth living. That's all there is to it" (*LKPP*, 17).

"Thinking things through" in the Socratic manner is closer to what we might call "ordinary" thinking—the kind of reflection all rational individuals are capable of—than it is to the activity practiced by "professional thinkers." From Arendt's perspective, the sin of many philosophers in the Western canon is that they construe thinking as a method or instrument for attaining *the* Truth. They see the value of reflection entirely in terms of its results—that is, in terms of its capacity to provide *answers* to questions about the nature of reality, the foundations of knowledge, the essence of morality, and the purpose of human life. Unlike "ordinary" thinking, which can be provoked by a wide range of phenomena, *philosophical* thinking in the West has largely focused on such "ultimate" questions. In Arendt's view, it has repeatedly and mistakenly subjected the reflective activity of reason to criteria more appropriate to the cognitive desire for knowledge than to the human quest for meaning.

What prompted the Western philosophers to reify the activity of thinking in the way that they did? Is there something in the experience of thinking that encourages not just withdrawal from the world, but the postulation of another world behind appearances? Does philosophical thinking reveal the "essence" of this mental activity in concentrated form, or does it distort and possibly pervert it?

The "stop and think" of ordinary reflection provides one clue to these questions. We can reflect on something only when we cease all doing; only, that is, when we withdraw—however briefly—from absorption in our daily activities and the world around us. Such withdrawal is the fundamental condition of all thinking, ordinary as well as philosophical. It seems obvious that the origins of Western philosophy's contemplative ideal are to be found in this thinking withdrawal, in the turning away from this world prompted by either the decline of polis life (as in Plato and Aristotle) or the replacement of the Roman Republic with the Empire's edifice of domination (the Stoics and early Christianity). "World alienation" thus lies at the root of the contemplative ideal and the attempt to turn the episodic "thinking withdrawal" into a way of life.

Turning away from *this* world prompts hopes that the inward turn of the philosopher, if pursued rigorously enough, might reveal a better or "True" one. Here another dimension of the thinking experience reveals its contribution to the rise of the "two-world" theories in Western philosophy after Plato. In reflection, we withdraw from the world of action and appearance into the quiet of an interior space where, through imagination and memory, we "de-sense" worldly phenomena and re-present them to ourselves. We are no longer caught up in the spectacle or surprise of specific actions or events, but can consider them more generally, thanks to the reflective distance provided by the "thinking withdrawal."

Thinking, then, is an invisible mental activity that deals with invisibles, with thought-things (concepts) that are clearly different in nature from the phenomenal particulars we encounter in the world. It is the invisibility of thought and its objects that led philosophers to make the fundamental distinction between essence and existence. The reification of this distinction provides the ground for all "two-world" metaphysical doctrines, all of which contrast the seemingly stable world of concepts (or "universals") with the coming and going of concrete particulars. The realm of essence, evidently available only to reason and the "eyes of the mind," is endowed with the character of immutable Being, while that of existence is reduced to the flux of all too mutable beings.

Another aspect of the thinking experience that contributes to the rise to the "two-world" metaphysics and the contemplative ideal in Western philosophy is its seeming timelessness. When we are absorbed in thought we cease all doing. We interrupt the temporal flow created by the things we started yesterday and what we hope to accomplish tomorrow. In its place, we have a small piece of non-time, the present, which, while usually fleeting, appears to expand itself indefinitely so long as we remain absorbed in thought and "out of time." The contemplative ideal underlying much of Western philosophy and religion is one that attempts to convert this small piece of non-time into a way of life. Thinking no longer denotes reflection on events and actions; it has become, instead, preparation for living in another world entirely, for extended communion with the eternal in an attitude of speechless wonder.

The reader may grant Arendt's point that there has been a pronounced tendency, in the Western tradition, to view the activity of thinking primarily as preparation for the "Truth" revealed by contemplation. But they may find themselves wondering, what's the harm in that?

The answer is twofold. First and most obviously, by making thinking into preparation for the revelation of a truth beyond words, Greek philosophy transformed thinking into a specialized activity. The assumption that only those who have turned their backs on the *vita activa* are able to authentically engage in thinking is one that serves to sharply distinguish the philosophical few from the apparently thoughtless many. This assumption runs directly counter to Arendt's suggestion (in TMC) that thinking may "condition men against evil-doing" by liberating their faculty of judgment from preconceived categories and prejudices. For that to be the case, "the faculty of thinking, as distinguished from the thirst for knowledge, must be ascribed to everybody; it cannot be a privilege of the few" (TMC, 166).

Second, this turning away from the world to pursue a higher Truth turns out to be temporary, since the thinker who has "beheld" the hidden order of Nature or the *kosmos* will want to *apply* that vision of eternal Being to the flux-filled realm of becoming. Ever since Plato converted the Ideas—originally, the beautiful, "that which shines forth most"—into standards for the realm of human affairs, philosophers have typically deduced practical and political philosophy from "first philosophy" (in the form of ontology or metaphysics) (*BPF*, 148).

This deductive habit of thought spread far beyond the relatively narrow precincts of philosophy. As Arendt points out in *OR*, even the American Founders, who discovered the power of mutual promising and acting together, felt compelled to cite a "higher law" to lend authority to their new constitutional creation. The notion that we cannot know what real justice is apart from such a transhuman reality or standard—originating in Plato, but spread throughout the Western world thanks to the triumph of

Christianity—has become virtually second nature to us. In its more aggressive versions (Plato's *Republic*, militant Christianity, Jacobin radicalism, totalitarian ideology), this recurring pattern of deducing coercive and violent political action from some supposedly unquestionable Absolute (Nature, God, History, etc.) has been the bane of Western civilization.

Arendt's probing of the ways the contemplative ideal has shaped our understanding of thinking as an activity thus has clear links back to her earlier investigations (in *THC*) with respect to how the traditional ranking of the *vita contemplativa* over the *vita activa* has perverted our understanding of action, effacing human plurality while framing political action as a means to some allegedly "higher" end. These parallels notwithstanding, the first volume of *LM* remains tightly focused on the activity of thinking itself. While Arendt draws on the "greats" of Western philosophy (Plato, Aristotle, et al.) for clues about its character, she is relentless in exposing the ways the contemplative ideal has distorted our understanding of it. What Bergson called the "habitual, normal, and banal act of our intellect" manifest in everyday reflection—what we might call "ordinary" thinking—is transformed into a specialized activity that only philosophers or other "professional thinkers" know how to practice.

As with *Thinking*, *Willing* examines one dimension of the life of the mind from a perspective that is at once descriptive and critical. Once again, Arendt turns to canonical philosophers for clues about the nature of this mental activity and the faculty (the Will) that underlies it. There is, however, a crucial difference. While philosophers have tended to apotheosize the faculty of reason behind thinking, they have been dubious about the Will, at least insofar as the latter is conceived as a faculty of "spontaneously beginning a new series of successive series or states" (Kant). The idea that human beings *have* such a capacity for spontaneous beginning has been repeatedly attacked by Western philosophy as an illusion. From a metaphysical point of view, acknowledging such a capacity would undercut the reign of the universal and the necessary (the "really real") and wind up identifying the human condition with a realm of unrelieved contingency and meaninglessness.

Thinking and the nature of reason have, of course, been topics of philosophical reflection ever since the pre-Socratics. However, when it comes to the mental activity of willing, we are confronted with a curious but unavoidable fact, namely, that "the faculty of the Will was unknown to Greek antiquity." It was discovered only as the result of experiences "about which we hear next to nothing before the first century of the Christian era" (*LM*, II, 3).

Arendt's claim about the historicity of the Will seems counterintuitive. However, others have noted it. As the philosopher Gilbert Ryle once observed, "Plato and Aristotle never mentioned [volitions] in their frequent and elaborate writings about the nature of the soul and the springs of conduct." For Ryle and many others, the Will was a "mere illusion of consciousness," and it is entirely understandable why the ancients preferred a moral psychology in which Reason commanded the other parts of the soul (Spirit and Desire) without any need to summon a separate faculty of volition (*LM*, II, 4).

Yet it is not entirely the case that there are no antecedents to the Will prior to the Christian era. As Arendt points out, in the *Metaphysics* Aristotle makes an important distinction between things that are necessarily and things that are only contingently. This distinction leads him to distinguish between the *substance* of a thing (its underlying reality) and its accidental attributes (such as color, taste, smell, etc.). Aristotle—and the Western tradition generally—takes it for granted that the reality of the necessary and substantial occupies a higher ontological plane than that of the "merely" accidental or contingent. And this, of course, has important consequences for how our philosophical tradition has viewed action and the realm of human affairs more generally.

Aristotle, however, did not leave it at this. Rather, he sees one human activity—fabrication or *poiēsis*—as bridging the gap between the realm of necessity and permanence and that of contingency and the ephemeral. Unlike the words and deeds that appear and just as quickly disappear in the realm of human affairs, the *products* of fabrication possess a clear durability and can be said to preexist potentially in the raw materials used by the artisan, as well as the vision of the finished product that guides him. A bronze bowl, for example, can be said to preexist its concrete actualization both in terms of its "material cause" (the ingot of bronze) and its "formal cause" (the idea of the bowl in the mind of the craftsman). But, as Arendt points out, this way of bridging the ontological chasm between the necessary and the contingent has, as its ultimate effect, the denial of genuine novelty. "The view that everything real must be preceded by a potentiality as one of its causes," Arendt writes, "implicitly denies the future as an authentic tense." We come to view the future as "nothing but a consequence of the past" (*LM*, II, 15).

However, while Aristotle's notion of the development of the potential into the actual (whether in nature or fabrication) renders the need for a faculty or organ for the future "entirely superfluous," he *does* supply what Arendt calls a "forerunner" of the Will with his notion of *proairesis*. Aristotle describes *proairesis* as the faculty that enables an individual to freely decide between two alternative courses of conduct. So conceived, *proairesis* clearly points the way to the traditional definition of the Will as *liberum arbitrium* or free choice. But neither Aristotle's *proairesis* nor the tradition's *liberum arbitrium* connotes anything like a power of spontaneously beginning.

Arendt's canvassing of the pre-Christian era for intimations of the Will (our "faculty for the future") thus yields a largely negative result. The best we can do is to affirm, with Aristotle, a faculty of free choice. It is only with the advent of the Christian era, and the replacement of the ancients' cyclical notion of time with a rectilinear one, that genuine novelty became a *conceptual* possibility. "The story that begins with Adam's expulsion from Paradise and ends with Christ's death and resurrection is a story of unique, unrepeatable events" (*LM*, II, 18). Moreover, the idea that human beings are made in the image of a creator God suggested that human beings might have a power to spontaneously begin, to transcend the "cycling years" of the ancients. Finally, the rise of Christianity resulted in a fundamental reconceptualization of the notion of *freedom*. What had previously been identified with an objective state of being (viz., the condition of the free republican citizen) was now identified with the believer's state of consciousness (*LM*, II, 19).

What the new imperative demands is a *voluntary* submission on the part of the believer, and Arendt thinks it is this aspect of the new Christian teaching that led to "the discovery of the Will"—that is, to the discovery of a faculty of *inner* freedom independent of all external constraints. Paradoxically, the discovery of this new faculty was made possible not by its power, but by its impotence. The "I will and *cannot*"—so different from the "I can" of the citizen who acts in concert with his fellows—is clearly expressed in St. Paul's statement, "For to will is present with me, but how to perform that which is good I find not." From the very beginning, the will is internally divided between the "I-will" and the "I-nil," a division that invariably arises as the Christian attempts to translate his good intentions into a consistent way of life.

Arendt traces the vicissitudes of this new faculty in the writings of Augustine, Aquinas, and Scotus. However, it is her account of "the main objections to the Will in post-medieval philosophy" that is most important. In early modern philosophy "there is an ever-recurring disbelief in the very faculty" of Will. Both Hobbes and Spinoza held that free will was an illusion, one born of the very structure of consciousness. In Spinoza's words, "men believe themselves to be free, simply because they are conscious of their actions, and unconscious of the causes whereby those actions are determined" (*LM*, II, 23). Subjective experience tells us that we are free. Objectively, however, we are as determined as anything else in the "mechanism of nature." So, while the Will might exist as a human faculty, we must acknowledge that the idea of an *undetermined* will is a non sequitur (or, as Hobbes put it, "absurd speech") (*LM*, II, 24).

While some post-Kantians gave the Will an unprecedented priority, for the most part "the suspicion of the willing faculty" remained a philosophical constant. Indeed, according to Arendt, Western philosophers were so scandalized by the idea that human beings possessed a capacity for spontaneous beginning that they continually sought ways to either deny freedom of the will (*à la* Hobbes and Spinoza) or demonstrate that new beginnings were actually the result of causal forces working "behind the backs" of the agents involved. The most famous instance of the latter is found in Hegel's philosophy of history. Through ingenious adaptation of the Aristotelian notions of potentiality and actualization, Hegel was able to present the course of World History as the continuous development of self-moving Spirit (*Geist*).

Hegel's retrospective glance (the "owl of Minerva" that takes flight only at dusk) returns us to the contemplative attitude of traditional philosophy, even though the object of contemplation is no longer the "order of the cosmos" or Nature, but History as a (meaningful) totality. Whatever persuasiveness it or more empirically grounded versions of "historical necessity" might have flows from the "reality effect" noted by the French philosopher Henri Bergson. "By virtue of its sheer factuality, reality throws its shadow behind it onto an infinitely distant past; thus it appears to have existed in the mode of potentiality in advance of its own actualization."

Arendt calls Bergson's observation "both elementary and highly significant." Yet despite its acuteness, it has played virtually no role in the "endless discussions of necessity versus freedom." Indeed, as Arendt sees it, "the original philosophical bias against contingency, particularity, and Will—and the predominance accorded to necessity, universality, and intellect—survived the challenge deep into the modern age." It survives still. Like its religious and metaphysical antecedents, modern philosophy has "found many different ways of assimilating the Will, the organ of freedom and the future, to the older order of things." Small wonder that Arendt finds herself in total agreement with Bergson when he states "most philosophers . . . are unable . . . to conceive of radical novelty and unpredictability" (*LM*, II, 32).

What is at the root of this inability? There is, of course, the traditional philosophical preference for a whole whose order and meaning can be contemplatively grasped by the intellect seeking *the* Truth. More concretely, there is the fundamental difference in tonality between the experience of the thinking ego and that of the willing ego. The former, familiar with withdrawal from the world and the "standing now" of reflection, inhabits a kind of enduring present, one free of the strife and cares of life. The latter is invariably oriented toward the future, to goals and projects the willing agent desires to achieve. The mood of the willing ego is not one of quiet and release from anxiety, but rather one of tension and uncertainty. The thinking ego yearns for release from the opposed pressures of past and future while the willing ego realizes that there is and can be no jumping out of time, no escape from temporality or the cares it imposes.

Readers of *Willing* may well assume that what one critic has called Arendt's "war on philosophical thinking" resolves itself in favor of elevating the Will over Reason, the future over the past, and action over thought. This assumption, however, is baseless. As we have seen, Arendt is hardly against *thinking*. What she criticizes is the idea that thinking is an activity reserved for a relative few. And, despite her critique of the philosophical tendency to be embarrassed by the idea of genuine novelty and to discount the "merely contingent," she is no voluntarist. She does not say, with Goethe's Faust, "in the beginning was the deed." Rather, what she upholds is the human capacity to interrupt history, to make new beginnings that no one could have predicted.

But what is this capacity grounded upon? When it comes to "grounding" a human capacity in a "faculty" supposedly possessed by the individual subject, Arendt is notably reticent. In part, this is because she shares Nietzsche and Heidegger's aversion to the very idea of a "ground," whether this is supposedly found in Nature or in human Reason or Will.

Yet the real reason lies elsewhere. True to her self-identification as a *political theorist* rather than a *philosopher*, she returns to the public-political realm: "The field where freedom has always been known, not as a problem, to be sure, but as a fact of human life, is the political realm" (*BPF*, 144). Some might see this as evading the question, but Arendt would demur. From her perspective, freedom is not a capacity lodged in the Will or any other "organ" of the individual. It is, rather, a reality made possible by the *fact* of human plurality and the *availability* of a public realm, one in which words never before said and deeds never before performed can occur.

This is not to say that the philosophers get it wrong, and that political thinkers and actors get it right. As Arendt notes in the last chapter of *LM*, even the men of the American Revolution were frightened by what she calls the "abyss of freedom." This fear led them to fall back upon either the Christian notion of divine providence or the Roman notion (expressed in Virgil's *Aeneid*) that every foundation is actually a *re-foundation*.

From Arendt's point of view, this is a lapse into what the existentialists called "bad faith," a turning away from the fact that it is human beings, bound together by "mutual promises," who are able to create new bodies politic and to commence entirely new stories. This capacity is “miraculous,” especially when compared to the repetitive behavior that characterizes much of everyday life. It is a miracle, however, that is made possible not by God but by political action— by plural agents “acting together, acting in concert” for the sake of a new beginning.

Further reading

Life and work

Elisabeth Young-Bruehl's biography of Arendt, *Hannah Arendt: For Love of the World* (New Haven, Yale University Press, 1982) is the standard account.

Hannah Arendt and Karl Jaspers, *Correspondence: 1926–1969* (New York, Harcourt, 1992).

Arendt's primary works—*The Origins of Totalitarianism* (New York, Harcourt, 1976), *The Human Condition* (Chicago, University of Chicago Press, 1958), *Between Past and Future* (New York, Penguin Classics, 2006), *On Revolution* (New York, Penguin Classics, 2006), *Eichmann in Jerusalem* (New York, Penguin Classics, 2006), *Men in Dark Times* (New York, Harcourt, 1968), *On Violence* (New York, Harcourt, 1970), *Crises of the Republic* (New York, Harcourt, 1972), and *The Life of the Mind* (New York, Harcourt, 1978)—are all in print.

Arendt's *Lectures on Kant's Political Philosophy* (ed. Ronald Beiner, Chicago, University of Chicago Press, 1984) contain material central to understanding her theory of moral and political judgment.

Jerome Kohn has edited several collections of Arendt's essays. These include *Essays in Understanding, 1930–1954* (New York, Harcourt, 1994), *Thinking Without a Bannister: Essays in Understanding 1953–1975* (New York, Schocken, 2018), and *Responsibility and Judgment* (New York, Schocken, 2003).

Political thought

George Kateb, *Hannah Arendt: Politics, Conscience, Evil* (Totowa, NJ, Rowman and Allanheld, 1984); Margaret Canovan, *Hannah Arendt: A Reinterpretation of her Political Thought* (Cambridge, Cambridge University Press, 1992); Dana Villa, *Arendt and Heidegger: The Fate of the Political* (Princeton, Princeton University Press, 1995); and Seyla Benhabib, *The Reluctant Modernism of Hannah Arendt* (Thousand Oaks, CA, Sage, 1996).

Collections of critical essays include *The Cambridge Companion to Hannah Arendt*, edited by Dana Villa (Cambridge, Cambridge University Press, 2000) and *Politics in Dark Times: Encounters with Hannah Arendt*, edited by Seyla Benhabib (Cambridge, Cambridge University Press, 2010).

Index

For the benefit of digital users, indexed terms that span two pages (e.g., 52–53) may, on occasion, appear on only one of those pages.

A

B

C

D

E

F

G

H

I

J

K

L

M

N

O

P

R

S

T

U

Antisemitism

A Very Short Introduction

Steven Beller

Antisemitism - a prejudice against or hatred of Jews - has been a chillingly persistent presence throughout the last millennium, culminating in the dark apogee of the Holocaust. This *Very Short Introduction* examines and untangles the various strands of antisemitism seen throughout history, from medieval religious conflict to 'new' antisemitism in the 21st century. Steven Beller reveals how the phenomenon grew as a political and ideological movement in the 19th century, how it reached it its dark apogee in the worst genocide in modern history - the Holocaust - and how antisemitism still persists around the world today.

BIOGRAPHY
A Very Short Introduction
Hermione Lee

Biography is one of the most popular, best-selling, and widely-read of literary genres. But why do certain people and historical events arouse so much interest? How can biographies be compared with history and works of fiction? Does a biography need to be true? Is it acceptable to omit or conceal things? Does the biographer need to personally know the subject? Must a biographer be subjective? In this *Very Short Introduction* Hermione Lee considers the cultural and historical background of different types of biographies, looking at the factors that affect biographers and whether there are different strategies, ethics, and principles required for writing about one person compared to another. She also considers contemporary biographical publications and considers what kind of 'lives' are the most popular and in demand.

> 'It would be hard to think of anyone better to provide a crisp contribution to OUP's Very Short Introductions.'
>
> **Kathryn Hughes, The Guardian**

www.oup.com/vsi

EXISTENTIALISM

A Very Short Introduction

Thomas Flynn

Existentialism was one of the leading philosophical movements of the twentieth century. Focusing on its seven leading figures, Sartre, Nietzsche, Heidegger, Kierkegaard, de Beauvoir, Merleau-Ponty and Camus, this *Very Short Introduction* provides a clear account of the key themes of the movement which emphasized individuality, free will, and personal responsibility in the modern world. Drawing in the movement's varied relationships with the arts, humanism, and politics, this book clarifies the philosophy and original meaning of 'existentialism' - which has tended to be obscured by misappropriation. Placing it in its historical context, Thomas Flynn also highlights how existentialism is still relevant to us today.

GERMAN PHILOSOPHY
A Very Short Introduction
Andrew Bowie

German Philosophy: A Very Short Introduction discusses the idea that German philosophy forms one of the most revealing responses to the problems of 'modernity'. The rise of the modern natural sciences and the related decline of religion raises a series of questions, which recur throughout German philosophy, concerning the relationships between knowledge and faith, reason and emotion, and scientific, ethical, and artistic ways of seeing the world. There are also many significant philosophers who are generally neglected in most existing English-language treatments of German philosophy, which tend to concentrate on the canonical figures. This *Very Short Introduction* will include reference to these thinkers and suggests how they can be used to question more familiar German philosophical thought.

Human Rights

A Very Short Introduction

Andrew Clapham

An appeal to human rights in the face of injustice can be a heartfelt and morally justified demand for some, while for others it remains merely an empty slogan. Taking an international perspective and focusing on highly topical issues such as torture, arbitrary detention, privacy, health and discrimination, this *Very Short Introduction* will help readers to understand for themselves the controversies and complexities behind this vitally relevant issue. Looking at the philosophical justification for rights, the historical origins of human rights and how they are formed in law, Andrew Clapham explains what our human rights actually are, what they might be, and where the human rights movement is heading.

www.oup.com/vsi

KEYNES

A Very Short Introduction

Robert Skidelsky

John Maynard Keynes (1883–1946) is a central thinker of the twentieth century, not just an economic theorist and statesman, but also in economics, philosophy, politics, and culture. In this *Very Short Introduction* Lord Skidelsky, a renowned biographer of Keynes, explores his ethical and practical philosophy, his monetary thought, and provides an insight into his life and works. In the recent financial crisis Keynes's theories have become more timely than ever, and remain at the centre of political and economic discussion. With a look at his major works and his contribution to twentieth-century economic thought, Skidelsky considers Keynes's legacy on today's society.

www.oup.com/vsi

CONSCIENCE

A Very Short Introduction

Paul Strohm

In the West conscience has been relied upon for two thousand years as a judgement that distinguishes right from wrong. It has effortlessly moved through every period division and timeline between the ancient, medieval, and modern. The Romans identified it, the early Christians appropriated it, and Reformation Protestants and loyal Catholics relied upon its advice and admonition. Today it is embraced with equal conviction by non-religious and religious alike. Considering its deep historical roots and exploring what it has meant to successive generations, Paul Strohm highlights why this particularly European concept deserves its reputation as 'one of the prouder Western contributions to human rights and human dignity throughout the world.

www.oup.com/vsi